# ANGOLA: A SYMPOSIUM
## VIEWS OF A REVOLT

# ANGOLA: A SYMPOSIUM
# VIEWS OF A REVOLT

*Issued under the auspices of the*
*Institute of Race Relations, London*

OXFORD UNIVERSITY PRESS

LONDON     NEW YORK     CAPE TOWN

1962

*Oxford University Press, Amen House, London, E.C.4.*

GLASGOW  NEW YORK  TORONTO  MELBOURNE  WELLINGTON
BOMBAY  CALCUTTA  MADRAS  KARACHI  LAHORE  DACCA
CAPE  TOWN  SALISBURY  NAIROBI  IBADAN  ACCRA
KUALA LUMPUR  HONG KONG

*Printed in Great Britain by R. J. Acford Ltd., Chichester*

# CONTENTS

# INTRODUCTION

IT is one of the objects of this series of books to provide background information about current happenings which in the daily Press often appear fragmentary and disconnected. The staff of the Institute have therefore tried to obtain a balanced and up-to-date account of the whole course of events in Angola by someone who is capable of finding and weighing evidence but who is not committed in advance to one point of view. In this we have proved unsuccessful. We have therefore decided to meet the need differently, by a symposium from different angles.

They are very different. There is a wide divergence about atrocities. But this may not be relevant to a historical view. Revolutions are not made on tea; even if a leader of revolt rejects this saying of Danton's, the anger which must be aroused if a people are to rise against their rulers can seldom be controlled; those who urge restraint are liable to the fate of Kerensky and the Gironde. But one may surely detest Marat without wanting to bring back the Bourbons; it is not rational to argue, or even to imply, that the dreadful things done by rebels in any way justify the system they are trying to upset. Indeed, the opposite argument, that they would not have done such things if they had nothing to rise against, is slightly the more sensible of the two—but neither are valid. The violence of the emotions on both sides in peasants' revolts, in slave risings, in India in 1857, in Matabeleland in 1896—these are not matters of reason, and the reactions do not vary with the strength of the provocation, as in a chemical experiment. In Angola, there is evidence of atrocities committed both by the rebels and by the Portuguese civilians in reprisal, and there is nothing inherently improbable in either set of accounts. These are things which both those who rebel and those who provoke the rebellion by refusal to reform ought to expect. How much they are exaggerated we may never know for certain; surely, it is more profitable for us in Britain to consider the factors on which British policy should be based.

It has been more difficult to obtain articles from supporters of Portuguese policy than from critics. This is partly because critics outnumber supporters, but also because official supporters, both in Britain and Portugal (who have been approached), are often hampered by considerations of secrecy and by the undesirability of committing a party or a government by their personal utterances. If some of the supporters seem to defend Portugal by attacking rebel atrocities, others appear to suggest that Portuguese colonial rule ought to continue because the Portuguese themselves are poor and not what we should call free. This too is hardly an argument. On the other hand, the critics seem on the whole indifferent to the frightful difficulties, and in particular the disunity, faced by countries suddenly independent, but in which free association in political parties and trade unions has not previously been possible. This has been perhaps as important a factor in the Congo's troubles as foreign interference and the lack of trained men. Miss Pinheiro's account of the political parties that have formed and re-formed leaves one doubtful of the possibility for a long time to come of sufficient African unity to run an independent nation, but at the same time sceptical about the Luso-African civilisation and that weather-beaten colonial sedative, that the heart of the people is sound and the rebellion has not spread. Everyone is conditioned by his own experience and I have heard this said too often and in too many different situations to have much faith in it. All these points, and particularly the disunity, are underlined by Mr. Matumona.

To read this collection of articles does not encourage optimism. It is hard to picture the Portugal of Dr. Salazar planning a peaceful transfer of power to African hands; no easier to picture Africans today contented with anything less than political power. But it is at least better to have this information than not.

It was inevitable in a collection of this kind that there should be some repetition and this has meant that in almost every article we have had to make editorial cuts. For these we apologise to the writers.

PHILIP  MASON

12 December 1961.

# SALAZAR'S PORTUGAL

## A. DE OLIVEIRA

THE tragic events which took place in Angola in February of 1961 have focused public attention on Portugal and on the Government of Dr. Salazar, who has been ruling the country since 1926.

For many years people in England had grown accustomed to the idea that even if the Portuguese regime did not abide by the rules of democracy it was at least a paternal dictatorship under the benevolent figure of Dr. Salazar. With certain misgivings that idea had been more or less accepted in this country, and with a few honourable exceptions, sedulously propagated by the British Press.

The curtain of silence that had fallen on Portuguese political life covered up the banning of all political parties, with the exception of Dr. Salazar's *União Nacional,* and hushed the news of the imprisonment of many of his opponents. In the meantime a steady flow of Portuguese official propaganda was being circulated throughout the world, giving a false and glamourised picture of his Corporate State. All this was being done through the care of the official bureau of propaganda, the *Secretariado Nacional de Informação,* that had been set up by Dr. Salazar himself and on which the Government lavished enormous sums. Periodicals and glossy magazines printed in French and English were and are still being sent to well-known foreign editors, to reporters, to high officials and, in general, to anyone who has ever expressed a wish to receive them. Gradually Dr. Salazar was trying to canvass world-wide public opinion and to seek a sympathy that his regime has never enjoyed. So when world opinion was startled by Captain H. Galvão's seizure of

A. DE OLIVEIRA is a Portuguese liberal.

the Portuguese liner *Santa Maria*, as well as by the revolt
that flared up in Luanda on the night of 4 February, the
great majority of the Portuguese people took the news
with excitement, but without surprise, considering those
new incidents further consequences of the repressive
measures and disastrous policies followed by Dr. Salazar
and his Government.

In point of truth nothing can be more erroneous and
misleading than the assumption that Dr. Salazar is a
benevolent dictator. A dictator he is indeed, by force and
by might, and not even his most lenient critic would
admit that he has ever been moved by any humanitarian
considerations in his dealings with opponents of his ideas
or of his regime. The reason for such a harsh suppression of all human rights must not be sought, as has been
done by a few foreign observers, in any particular
propensity or failing in the Portuguese Premier's
character, but in the essence and the ethics of the
Corporate State, or 'New State', which came into being
by a military *putsch* in May 1926. Inspired by the same
political ideas as the autocratic regimes of Hitler and
Mussolini, the New State rallied the most reactionary and
conservative elements in Portuguese society, who feared
the badly needed social reforms that the young Republic,
established in 1910, was planning in a tentative way to put
into effect. The generous liberalism of the Republican
leaders made them underestimate the mood of the
supporters of the old regime, who, after they had sworn
allegiance to the Republican constitution, were left
unharmed and undisturbed in the posts which they held
before the revolution. Fearing the loss or the curtailment
of their privileges, the discontented took advantage of
their position, and gathering strength in some army
quarters they took power by force. This *coup d'état* was
preceded by a period of terrorist activity very similar to
that which is at the moment taking place in France and
Algeria.

In contrast, during the thirty-six years of Salazar's rule not one single act of the same kind has ever been attributed to the Opposition. Yet during the sixteen years of the Portuguese Republic, abortive military revolts, led by people with close political affinities with Dr. Salazar were rife.[1] This period of political instability slyly fostered by Dr. Salazar's supporters, was to be used later as an argument in favour of the dictatorship, since the parliamentary system 'had proved' inadequate to the temperament of the Portuguese people.

Once in power, one of the first measures taken by Dr. Salazar was to establish the Secret Police, the *Polícia Internacional e de Defesa do Estado* (International and State Defence Police) better known as PIDE, which resembles in organisation and methods Hitler's *Gestapo*. And unfortunately this is not just a casual comparison drawn for the sake of stylistic clarification. The headquarters of PIDE are in Lisbon, but from there the Secret Police extends its influence to the whole of Portugal and colonies through a network of branches which operate in the main towns. The PIDE can rely entirely on the police force (*Polícia Judiciária* and *Polícia de Segurança Pública*) as well as on the *Guarda Nacional Republicana*, a special military body well equipped for street battle. The *Guarda Fiscal*, an armed force of customs officers, is also another strong ally of PIDE.

The powers of the Secret Police are virtually absolute and anyone who opposes the regime is liable to a long period of imprisonment without trial. The suspect may also be tortured. Interference with the rights of the defence lawyers is also a common feature in the trials of Portuguese democrats.

The treatment given to political prisoners is not in keeping with the official regulations which are observed in jails where there are prisoners serving a sentence for a breach of common law. Many of the old prisons, like the Aljube in Lisbon, have had their façade white-washed and repaired, but the conditions inside are appalling. In the

old forts of Caxias and Peniche, which at one time kept
a silent watch over the Portuguese coast, there are damp
dungeons where hundreds of patriots spend months and
even years.

Some of the prisoners have been jailed for reasons
which in England would be considered quite trivial, as it
is the case with Nuno Duarte, arrested and prosecuted
because he wrote the word 'Peace' on a wall. It is also
known that the Portuguese Secret Police does not hesitate
to use more expedient methods to get rid of some
opponents of Dr. Salazar's regime. Alfredo Diniz, a metal
worker, was shot on 4 July 1945 on a road near Lisbon by
a PIDE agent. Dr. Ferreira Soares, from near Espinho,
met the same fate in his surgery on 4 July 1942 at the
hands of two PIDE agents.[2]

In this harsh way Dr. Salazar has tried to silence all
opposition to his regime. By imposing strict measures on
the freedom of expression and individual rights, by using
the fact that someone has shown any political sympathies
for the Opposition, Dr. Salazar can deprive any Portuguese
citizen from obtaining a diploma that would enable him
to practise a profession. Yet no one can be admitted into
the Civil Service, which in Portugal includes all teachers
in state schools and in the universities, if he or she does
not sign a declaration of total submission to the regime.

One of the immediate results of such legislation was
the great purge of 1945, which deprived the country of
some of its best scientists and academics who lost their
posts and were forced to seek a new occupation which
more often than not had nothing to do with their learning
and skill.

This persecution of intellectuals had been preceded, was
followed, and is still vigorously maintained by censorship
of the Press, which is only reduced for very brief periods
during an election campaign, as happened recently during
the election of deputies to the National Assembly. But
even a small measure of freedom of the Press serves as
indirect aid to PIDE, which will know the opponents of

the regime who are courageous enough to sign public manifestos.

In such circumstances free elections are virtually impossible and that is the main reason why the Opposition feels compelled to withdraw its candidates from the electoral contest, as it did in the November elections. The Government claims the right to delete from the electoral roll any candidate whom it does not favour. No possible arguments can be used to defend this electoral fraud, despite the strenuous efforts of some Portuguese journalists who try to win the approval of foreign opinion. In the colony of Mozambique, when it appeared that the candidates of the Opposition were gathering strong support, the elections were promptly cancelled.

Having eliminated any sort of organised opposition to the regime, Dr. Salazar set himself the task of securing his own position and that of his Government. For that purpose he formed in 1936 a praetorian guard which came into existence under the name of 'Portuguese Legion' (*Legião Portuguesa*). The members of this militia were recruited on a voluntary basis among police informers and a small group of enthusiasts who saw in it a good opportunity of ingratiating themselves with their superiors.

The 'Portuguese Legion' has a special branch, the 'Territorial Civil Defence' (*Defesa Civil do Território*) and is thus enabled to exert full authority all over the country. In the case of an emergency declared by the Government it can act as a repressive force. For the time being it has control of the activity of individuals and institutions. The Legion is armed, has a special green uniform and is submitted to regular military drilling. In practice it supplies the Security shield to the National Union to which some of the militiamen belong. Together with the 'Portuguese Youth' (*Mocidade Portuguesa*), an organisation formed in 1936 in which school boys and girls are forcibly enrolled, the Legion provides a hard core of supporters who conform in doctrine and action to the principles of Dr. Salazar's New State.[3] The fighting temper of the 'Legion' has never been tested, since the 'subversives' were a legal fiction created to justify its existence. On the whole this complex and solid security system headed by the Secret Police (PIDE), which is only responsible to itself and Dr. Salazar, has proved to be the most efficient barrier against the protest and the often expressed wish for freedom of the Portuguese people. It has served admirably the ideas of Dr. Salazar regarding elections and universal suffrage, a subject on which he has voiced his views:

I do not believe in universal suffrage, because the individual vote does not take into account human differentiation. I do not believe in equality but in hierarchy. Men, in my opinion should be equal before the law, but I believe it is dangerous to attribute to all the same political rights.[4]

These words of Dr. Salazar deserve a detailed analysis because they reveal political ideas which have been the true inspiration of the small group of financiers, Army and Navy officers who support him. When Dr. Salazar took power, the fraction of the Portuguese upper classes that backed the *coup d'état* lacked a political philosophy. This Dr. Salazar has provided, shaping the country to the wishes of the privileged few. When Dr. Salazar asserted 'I do not believe in equality but in hierarchy', he had laid down the cornerstone on which his political system is built. And herein lies the deep sense of discrimination which begins in Portugal itself and is extended to the Portuguese territories. This is one of the most important aspects to be considered in a symposium on racial discrimination.

Discrimination is enforced in a much more subtle way than the one which we are used to see or to hear about. It avoids the more spectacular aspects and the obvious manhunt which may easily move our anger and cause abhorrence. Yet when faced with the need for more drastic measures, once the silent segregation has failed, there is no doubt that the authorities and Portuguese white settlers are capable of provoking ugly scenes, as we have witnessed in the Luanda incidents. That is also why any study on discrimination in the Portuguese colonies must start from an enquiry into the situation inside Portugal itself.

The defenders of the Portuguese colonial regime and the Portuguese authorities prided themselves frequently on the fact that Portugal had never had any trouble in its overseas possessions. But it was only due to a severe curtain of silence that unrest inside Portugal and colonies could be kept secret. The general strike of 1934, and the strikes of the forties and the unsuccessful revolts of army officers in 1946 and 1947 would suffice to prove that there was always discontent and agitation in the metropolis itself. A callous attitude to legitimate grievances on the part of Dr. Salazar's Government was bound to lead sooner or later to acts of violence. By its systematic refusal to negotiate with the Angolan leaders, the Portuguese Government made itself responsible for the colonial war.

Inside metropolitan Portugal Dr. Salazar's concept of hierarchy operates in practice a sharp economic differentiation between a small minority of the 'great families' and the broad mass of the population. It is not a discrimination imposed by colour but by property. In order to qualify as an elector every literate adult must submit proof of high educational attainment or that he pays a certain minimum in taxes. Since more than 40 per cent of the population is illiterate and since Portugal has the lowest annual income per head in Europe, it is clear that only a minority is entered in the electoral register. But even then if there is any suspicion that the elector may cast his vote for the Opposition candidate, his name will swiftly be deleted from the electoral roll. Moreover, the number of those who are considered literate is in fact much smaller that the statistics admit. Many of them leave primary schools at the age of ten, and, forced by economic hardship go back to the poor rural districts where they have come from. There they have no reading facilities and gradually they forget the little they have learned.

The son or the daughter of a Portuguese industrial worker who earns an average wage of £1 14s. 0d. a week, or the

children of peasants who depend on seasonal labour to
receive daily wages ranging from two shillings for women
and five shillings for men, will never have the chance of
going to the secondary schools.  Therefore the admission
to secondary-school education is limited by economic
factors.  Some students—and only a very small minority—
may be exempted from paying school fees, but in view of
the low income of their parents only a small number can
really continue their studies.  Consequently the number of
those who graduate from the university is far below the
needs of Portugal itself, to say nothing of the vast empire
that demands a high flow of intellectual resources.  In
the universities, in scientific institutions and research
centres under government control, the enrolment of
scientific workers is made under the surveillance of the
PIDE which on the slightest suspicion cuts short academic
careers.  If, despite everything, a teacher gets as far as this,
he cannot be made a professor without the final approval
of the Council of Ministers.

Such a system leads up naturally to a *caste* differentiation
which makes a mockery of Portuguese civil law.  Almost
every Portuguese knows one or two incidents in which the
law has been flouted by the so-called hierarchy.  If, for
example, on infringing a traffic regulation a member of
the hierarchy makes himself known to the officer in charge,
he will be dismissed on the spot with apologies.  There
are even cases in which a more courageous police officer
in the fulfilment of his duties has been transferred from
the capital to a provincial town for ignoring the tacit rules
of the game.

But who are in fact the people who form Dr. Salazar's
hierarchy?  Since confessed political allegiance and submission have taken the place of scientific ability and
firmness of character, we are left with those who benefit
in one way or another from the economic policy pursued
by Dr. Salazar and his ministers.

Once again official statistics will throw some light on
the subject.  Portugal is a country where 50 per cent of

the population make a living from the land. However, the property system shows unbalanced distribution of the culti-vated areas. Four of the greatest landlords in the country own between them 235,000 acres of land, which is the same amount as held by 50,400 small farmers.[5] These landlords can impose their will by fixing market prices for farm produce through the respective department (*grémio*) of the corporative system. They may ruin small competitors who are forced to sell to the *grémio* their own produce. The *grémio* will then sell at the most profitable price. This is just one example of how the corporate system works. Naturally the great landowners are staunch supporters of the regime. So also, even if not so enthusi-astic, are the many officials of the corporate organisation who fear for their daily bread.

In the industrial field Dr. Salazar has encouraged and protected the monopolies.[6] They operate inside Portugal itself and in the colonies. The CUF and the SACOR are two of the richest and most powerful combines which own practically the whole country and have solid interests in Angola and Mozambique. Through a vast network of banks they control many sections of the Portuguese economy. The monopolists and Navy and Army officers who, either in active service or on reaching retiring age, may be offered a seat on the board of any one of these companies as a reward for their loyalty to the regime, are the people who back Dr. Salazar. Professor Adriano Moreira, the Minister for Overseas Territories, attached to the Sonefe and the Standard Electric, finds himself now in an ideal position to favour a wider penetration into the colonies of national monopolies and foreign investments. The new supreme commander of the Portuguese Legion, Henrique Tenreiro, is one of the great magnates of industry and finance in the country. This is the caste and the hierarchy in which Dr. Salazar believes. It is not a hier-archy of intellect but rather an oligarchy of plutocrats.

Dr. Salazar hates publicity because he fears that it might unveil the truth about his regime. He has done so much

to boost the New State that the present events in Angola
have had the effect of a catastrophe. Everyone feels, even
the official Portuguese Propaganda Bureau, that things are
no longer the same and that world public opinion feels only
revulsion for Dr. Salazar's regime.

For almost thirty-five years he succeeded in convincing
a few statesmen that, due to what he called the 'uniqueness'
of the Portuguese case, his dictatorship was the best form of
government for the Portuguese people. Now it is obvious
that he has not solved any of the most pressing national
problems and that his policies are becoming a real cause
for alarm. But he succeeded, however, in creating a dictatorship of a new kind in which his professorial sleight-of-hand
played a major role. By issuing cleverly written decrees
at appropriate strategic moments, when the world was too
busy with international problems or too indifferent to care
about the fate of small nations, he has given the dictatorship
its true character.

Deeply sensitive to the mood of international opinion,
Dr. Salazar fears any accurate report on Portuguese life or
any adverse criticism of the regime that appears in printed
form. Whenever a foreign book which is even mildly
critical of his administration is shown in Portuguese book-
shops the Secret Police wastes no time in seizing it.
Sensitivity towards foreign criticism reaches a particularly
high pitch if it comes from either the United States or
England. England is regarded as the traditional old ally
and the reactions of British public opinion have an
immediate reflection on the political barometer of
Portuguese life. For the Portuguese liberals, England still
appears as a bastion of freedom, a country where the
institutions they praise are still flourishing and where their
forefathers sought asylum in the early nineteenth century.
Any condemnation of Dr. Salazar's policy is a gain for
the Portuguese democrats. It assists indirectly those forces
which are trying to change the present trend of events inside
Portugal. The support given by world public opinion to
the Portuguese democrats is, in fact, much more than a

symbolic gesture of human solidarity, for it can have positive and palpable results.

It may be all very well for Dr. Salazar and his ministers to make military plans and talk about keeping the overseas territories by force, but Portuguese economy, already shaken by Dr. Salazar's austerity measures, is not geared to war and will not be able to sustain the prolonged effort that the colonial campaign in Angola will demand. In fact, this is one of the greatest weaknesses of the regime and reveals the truth about Dr. Salazar's much lauded achievements as an economist.

By cutting drastically the standard of living of the Portuguese people, which in some cases is below the subsistence level, Dr. Salazar has reduced inflation and made the escudo a sound currency in the international market. Yet to balance the country's finances Dr. Salazar has to rely heavily on the colonies. The tourist trade, the remittances from Portuguese living abroad and the inflow of foreign capital, which in turn harms the country's independence, are insufficient to cover the annual foreign trade deficit. This amounts to roughly two-thirds of the total state revenue. Dr. Salazar eases off the deficit by making the colonies pay for it. This is the only way in which he has succeeded in presenting each year an apparently sound budget. The colonies are, therefore, more than a necessity for Dr. Salazar. But Salazar himself would have to admit that the Portuguese economy is parasitic. In 1959 Portugal's deficit in its balance of trade with the world was over £53 million. In the balance of trade of Angola and Mozambique Portuguese exports pay less than half of the imports. Indeed these imports from Portugal do not correspond to the true needs of the colonies but are made in order to favour the economy of the mother country. In 1958, 10 per cent of the total amount of Portuguese exports to Angola consisted of wine.[7] It is only by imposing special provisions for Portuguese imports in the colonies, as well as by granting vast and new concessions to foreign capital, that Dr. Salazar finds the necessary funds to avert total disaster. At the same time the figures for the balance of trade among the Portuguese colonies themselves are very low. In Angola, for example, the imports from other Portuguese possessions are practically negligible.[8] These hard facts will help us understand that there is no point in issuing new decrees, as Dr. Salazar is doing now under the pressure of the Angolan war, unless there is a basic change in the economic structure. And this is as far off as ever.

At home Dr. Salazar has embarked on what he likes to call a planned economy. But his development plans have proved a resounding failure. The targets set for the first plan were never reached, and from data gathered by the 'Higher Inspection for the execution of the Second Plan of Development', a special bureau created by Dr. Salazar, things are far from good. Heavy industry is 65 per cent under the mark set in the plan. Railways, rolling stock, airports and technical research have received under 75 per cent of the planned estimates.

In 1960 only 32·8 per cent of the amount envisaged for the whole year has been invested. In agriculture the results are also disastrous. Although 50 per cent of the Portuguese people make a living out of the land, the index of production in 1960 has only increased by 2·7 per cent since 1947.

There is no doubt now that the Second Plan of Development will meet the fate of the first one. The colonial war is undermining Portuguese economy. In the general budget for 1961, £49 million was allocated to the armed forces and to the Secret Police. If one takes into account the fact that the Government spends a little less than £64 million on the whole of the public and social services, including education, one may understand the hardships that the Portuguese people are facing at the moment. It must also be borne in mind that in Portugal there is no free health service.[9] The impoverishment of the broad masses of the population is an inescapable truth. Inflation is rising. In the last six months the country's reserves were down from £251 to £212 million, while the circulation of paper

money in the same period has risen from £175 million to
to £203 million.[10]

This situation is a cause of grave concern for the Opposition. In the November elections it was forced once again
to abstain, but it made a strong stand against the colonial
war, and in declarations released to the Press has agreed on
a policy of self-determination for the colonies. Hitherto
only the banned Portuguese Communist Party had advo-
cated, since the early fifties, the right to independence and
self-determination for the Portuguese colonies. The national
unity of the Opposition is a serious blow for Dr. Salazar.
For the first time it comprehends all the democratic forces
inside Portugal, including liberals, monarchists, Catholics,
and left-wing parties. This united front against Dr. Salazar
and the New State believes in legal, semi-legal and illegal
means to change the present regime. In this way it has
formed an underground organisation the 'Joint Committee
for Patriotic Action, (*Junta de Acção Patriótica*), which
issues its own paper, *Tribuna Livre* (*Free Press*). This
looks very much like one of the resistance tracts published
under the Nazi occupation of France. In it the Portuguese
democrats criticise Dr. Salazar's policies and condemn the
colonial war in Angola.

Together with this struggle for freedom and democracy
there is also an open campaign for a general and complete
amnesty for all Portuguese political prisoners and exiles.
The policy of a wage freeze, too, is encountering a stronger
and firmer opposition by the working class and all
professional employees. Inflation is lowering their already
poor standard of living and wide military conscription—
some estimates give a figure of 80,000 men in arms—is
depriving many families, particularly in the rural districts,
of their wage-earners. Naturally all this is causing discontent
and in army barracks, such as at Évora and Setúbal, the
conscripts with the support of the local population have
refused to leave for Angola.

The Portuguese people do not get any benefits from
colonial exploitation. In order to reduce the high number

of unemployed Dr. Salazar has always encouraged emigration to the colonies. But the peasants who settle in the
overseas territories are in general illiterate or semi-literate
people with no knowledge of the local conditions. Having
no adequate technical training, which would enable them
to cultivate properly the new land, they fall back on their
traditional techniques, which in many cases were not even
the most efficient at home, and in a short time they are in
debt. Crops are lost and many of them have to give up
the land altogether. To avert the sad picture of the failure
of the white man, the authorities usually try to offer the
best land to the immigrant, at the expense of its African
owner who may be expelled at any time. At Cela and in
the Limpopo Valley in Angola the authorities have established white colonies *into which no African is admitted*.
Some immigrants, who in spite of all this assistance do
not succeed in making a living out of the land, look for
adventure elsewhere and become small shopkeepers in
outlandish posts.

The big monopolies, however, make huge profits, and
the wealth of Angola is being drained from the country
and into the pockets of a few Europeans.

It is by resorting to old texts such as the essentially
bellicose national epic, *The Lusiads,* which deals extensively
with the exploits of the Portuguese conquerors of the late
fifteenth century and expresses all the crusading spirit of the
past, that the New State tries to justify its colonial policy.
The Portuguese may never have indulged in racial discrimination to the extent that other Powers have done. They
may have been at times less ruthless than other colonial
Powers, but there is no doubt that history as written in
Portuguese textbooks is very different from reality. No
serious and impartial historian would agree that there
has been a generally consistent policy of racial equality for
all Portuguese colonies.

Dr. Salazar will never win the war in Angola, nor will his
'new look' colonial policy succeed in bringing peace to
a troubled area. How can anyone believe that he is going

to give the Africans the rights which he has denied to the Portuguese at home? Besides, the facts speak for themselves. It is all very well for Dr. Salazar to abolish by decree the old differentiation that divided the Africans into 'civilised' and 'uncivilised' inhabitants; but this will not give them the literacy and property qualifications which would entitle them to vote in Angola, where, according to the 1958 census, 99·6 per cent of the African population were illiterate.

It is quite clear both to the Opposition and to the African leaders that the present grave situation inside Portugal and in the territories under Portuguese domination is the result of thirty-five years of Dr. Salazar's rule. The leaders of the nationalist movement in Angola have often repeated that they are not at war with the Portuguese people, but with the repressive forces of Dr. Salazar's new brand of colonialism. Many Portuguese have suffered and died because they have demanded freedom and democracy for Portugal. Many have been imprisoned for voicing their approval of Angola's right to independence. Dr. Salazar answers all these charges with the brutality of PIDE and by establishing a new concentration camp in Missombo, Angola. The facts are there for everyone to judge. In this final struggle against Dr. Salazar's regime, the peoples of Portugal and of the colonies are allies, not enemies. Together they will bring freedom and democracy to their respective countries, and rid themselves of a dictatorship that history will one day judge with the greatest severity.

## NOTES

[1] Peter Fryer and Patricia McGowan Pinheiro, *Oldest Ally : A Portrait of Salazar's Portugal*, London, Dennis Dobson, 1961, p. 113.

[2] A. Ramos, 'Political Repression under Salazar', *Portuguese and Colonial Bulletin*, vol. 1, April 1961, p. 20.

[3] António de Figueiredo, *Portugal and its Empire : the Truth*, London, Victor Gollancz, 1961, p. 43.

[4] *The Observer*, 29 August 1954 ; *The Times*, 21 May 1959.

[5] A. Ramos, op. cit., p. 2.

[6] Dr. Ralph von Gersdorf, *Massnahmen zur Förderung der Privaten Kapitalbildung im Portugiesischen Reich,* Zurich, Polygraphischer Verlag AG, 1958, p. 165.

[7] 'Rapport sur le Colonialisme Portugais, 1960', *Tam-Tam,* April–May, 1961, p. 96.

[8] Armando Nogueira, 'Fisionomia e Evolução do Comércio Externo de Angola', *Ultramar,* vol. I, January–February 1961.

[9] Data taken from the *Boletim de Informação do Banco de Fomento Nacional,* Lisbon, 1961. See also G. Araujo, 'Salazar's Economy of War', *Portuguese and Colonial Bulletin,* vol. I, June–July 1961, pp. 39–40.

[10] Colin Legum, 'Salazar Smashes Demonstrations', *The Observer,* 12 November 1961.

# THE TWO FACES OF PORTUGAL

## ANDREW MARSHALL

WHENEVER I return to Portugal I feel that I am not just in another country, I feel somehow that I have gone back to another age. There is the unreality of an old picture post-card about it all. But there is also the feel of tragedy.

Autumn is perhaps the loveliest season to visit Portugal. In the countryside it is a time for celebration, of fairs and of dancing in streets lit by flares and paper lanterns to the whistle, tinkle and thump of a village band. In the wine-country, even when the vintage has long since passed, the scent of must still hangs heavy in the air. The Portuguese peasant, although he earns very little, is in some ways among the more fortunate of his countrymen. For one thing, he can grow at least his basic food. But the land is often poor and he is essentially a subsistence farmer.

In the more distressed areas, and one finds them in almost every region of Portugal, standards of living are among the lowest in Europe. Winter means unemployment and even greater hardship; so once a year, when the autumn comes, the peasants celebrate, almost defiantly, and the rich Portuguese and the foreign tourists come to watch; and go away, particularly the foreigners, with a comfortable feeling, tinged perhaps with envy: these are a simple people and obviously poor, yet how contented they all seem. But few foreigners return a month or two later when the fairs are over and the decorations and the paper lanterns have

ANDREW MARSHALL was Reuter's correspondent in Portugal after the war, and then in Brazil and South America. He became the South American correspondent of *The Times* in 1950 and at the end of 1958 joined the editorial staff in London. He resigned in April 1961 to be a freelance journalist and radio commentator. Mr. Marshall has written many articles and given numerous talks on South American and Iberian affairs.

been packed away for another year. The Portuguese peasant celebrates the autumn much as a carnival, a prelude to a harsh Lent.

But for the Portuguese in the towns the change of season is not a festive occasion. One of the first warnings of approaching winter are advertisements in the newspapers of ways to seal up windows, for the average Portuguese household can afford little in the way of heating. Electricity and fuel are costly and ordinary Portuguese make do with a reeking oil-stove or shallow copper bowls filled with embers and sand which look charming but hardly seem to give enough heat to excite an automatic fire alarm at three paces. When winter sets in, the family goes to bed early and with all their clothes on. Another sign of the approaching cold is the row of anxious women looking hopelessly into the windows of back-street second-hand clothes shops and pawnbrokers.

This is a country of paradox and startling contrasts and nowhere can one see the two faces of Portugal, the opulence and the squalor, more distinctly than in Lisbon. 'Pretty' is a word which comes instinctively to one's mind when one arrives there. This is a terraced city of gardens with houses painted in every pastel shade, of pink and green, of cream and blue, so crisp and clean that it reminds one of an advertisement for a detergent. The tidy streets, the teeming traffic, the shining new cars and the London-type double-decker buses, all seem to be part of a game of make-believe. Inexplicably, one feels that even the traffic policemen standing under gay, striped umbrellas on tubs which surely must have been borrowed from a circus ring, should not be directing traffic at all. They should be selling candy floss. Lisbon somehow still manages to retain the atmosphere of a village. But behind the façade there is another Lisbon, of slums and shabby alleyways; of whole streets without any real sanitation and where one tap in the open is the only water supply for an entire row of houses.

In the past few years there has been a building boom in Portugal, for, next to foreign shareholdings, rich Portuguese seem to have pinned their faith now on bricks and mortar. Modern blocks of flats, hotels and luxury villas seem to be going up everywhere. The Government itself has built whole new districts. Yet one of the biggest problems the ordinary Portuguese faces in Lisbon, or any other of the larger towns, is housing he can afford. Many of these privately-built blocks of flats are half empty. They were built as a tangible investment, much in the same way as the peasant of the Alentejo and the Algarve keeps his hoard of a few sovereigns hidden in the most unlikely places. Although the escudo is still one of the hard currencies of the world, Portuguese with money are wondering how long it will stay that way.

For most ordinary Portuguese, even the flats and the housing estates which the Government is building provide no solution. These are usually reserved for minor civil servants and their friends and relations. In Salazar's Portugal, to serve the regime has its carefully-scaled rewards. With cheap accommodation and other benefits, a policeman, for example, has a far easier life than a fairly senior clerk in an office. For many Portuguese, a solution to the housing problem is to share, often not a house but a set of rooms, with sometimes two or three other families.

It is misleading to attempt to draw a comparison between costs, wages and conditions of life in Portugal with those in any other European country, except perhaps for parts of Spain and southern Italy; the Portuguese way of life is in some ways unique. What can be said is that the average Portuguese is poorly recompensed. The price he is having to pay for Dr. Salazar's tidy economics is high. A labourer or even a lower-paid office worker often has to seek part-time work in addition to his regular job, which may mean his having to work anything up to fifteen hours a day, six or even seven days a week. A serious illness in his family can spell disaster, for he enjoys virtually no social security. For the education of his children the State provides four years' free schooling from the age of seven. It was only in 1960 that this provision was extended to girls. But because of the shortage of schools and teachers a child receives, on average, three to four hours' schooling a day. For the great mass of Portuguese children this is the only education they will ever get.

After thirty years of the Salazar regime, which set out to create a model co-operative state, life for the average Portuguese has changed little. Portugal always has been and still is a country with a rigid class structure, almost a set piece of Victoriana. At the top is a very rich and very small uncompromisingly conservative class, which, with the full blessing of the regime, executes the control of the economic life of the country and of the overseas territories. At the bottom is the great mass of the Portuguese, hard-working, poorly paid, with no voice in the country's affairs and apparently apathetically philosophical about it all. Wedged in between is a somewhat indistinct middle class, frustrated, ashamed, and worried by this continued brazen disparity of lots. It is from their ranks that the sincere and thinking critics of the Salazar regime come; and many of them today are in jail on charges of treason.

Although over the years the basic cost of living has not increased in the same way as it has in some other parts of Europe, wages, except for civil servants, have remained virtually frozen. Since the revolt, prices and indirect taxation have been rising and many Portuguese today are feeling the pinch very badly indeed. Conditions for factory workers are rather better, but this type of worker is in a minority, for Portuguese industry is still in its infancy. Some of the larger industries are showing a far greater concern for the welfare of their workers than commercial and agricultural employers, but in some ways the Portuguese factory worker is subject to even more rigid political discipline than any other class of employee. Admittedly, it is in the very few industrial areas of the country that the influence of Communism has become more evident; and the result is that any apparently organised demand for better wages or conditions is promptly branded as Communist-inspired. What happens then is that the management simply withdraws and the police take over; there are no unions and striking is, in effect, a penal offence. Certainly some of the people who have attempted to organise 'labour revolts' have been Communists; but in Portugal, to be branded as a Communist, or even a Communist dupe, which in the eyes of the law can sometimes be worse, has become the occupational hazard of almost any reformer, however well intentioned.

One of the more disturbing aspects of the Salazar regime is that its supporters seem to derive a sense of security and comfort very simply from dismissing even its moderate critics, who are sincerely worried about the future, as either Communist tools or people labouring under hallucinations. It is this supreme confidence that they can resist even a breath of change that has involved Portugal in a costly and seemingly hopeless colonial war in Angola and there is every likelihood of uprisings in the other Portuguese territories, such as Mozambique and Portuguese Guinea. But the Portuguese do not think of themselves as fighting a colonial war; nor do they seem to feel that it may be a hopeless one. They claim that what they are fighting is international Communism. They do not regard the outburst in Angola, for example, as due to African nationalism. They call it foreign aggression.

Although the native population of these African territories, particularly Angola, have even greater reason now to hate the presence of the Portuguese, the Portuguese blandly ascribe this unrest and bitterness to the agitation of international Communism. Yet it is not only the African native who is rebelling. Portuguese settlers also have some pretty deep grievances against what they regard as Lisbon's exploitation of their efforts. The Portuguese overseas territories account for about a third of Portugal's gross national income. Yet the conditions of life in much of these territories are very low indeed. Many settlers now feel that economic exploitation is by no means a harsh description of Portuguese administration. It is the same situation, although to a far lesser degree, as that which

lost Portugal Brazil 140 years ago. To Lisbon's mind,
that Portuguese settlers should be restive is bad enough,
but that the Portuguese Africans, inspired by the emerging
African states, should now be revolting, is regarded as
downright impertinence.

When the first rumbles began to be heard in Angola,
a Portuguese friend in Lisbon summed up the attitude of
the Salazar regime in this way. 'Our Government,' he
said, 'will stand no nonsense from the Africans or any-
body else. The pattern of life which we have designed
for the African is the best suited to his needs and temperament. These people must be forced to work and an
occasional flogging never did anyone any harm. And',
he added wickedly, 'why should the African complain?
This same policy is followed here in Portugal too, isn't it?'

To understand Portugal's outlook towards these overseas
territories, one must realise that it is not simply cynicism
which prompts the Portuguese to describe Angola, for
instance, not as a colony but as a Province, as much a
part of Portugal as the island of Madeira. They regard
their right to remain in Africa as inalienable. They have
been there centuries longer than any other colonial power;
furthermore, so they argue, their colonial policy is unique.
They do not have racial prejudices. Portuguese peasants
settle in Angola and Mozambique, marry natives and work
side by side with the Negro. They explain that Portugal,
however, is a poor country and cannot do as much for
the African native as she would like to. The problem, they
add, is precisely the same at home. The Salazar regime
does not have the resources to fight, for example, tuber-
culosis and illiteracy; and Portugal has one of the highest
incidences of both in Western Europe. Salazar's policy,
these same Portuguese will tell you, is to keep the people,
including the Portuguese African, reasonably contented,
but above all, disciplined. In Angola, they will assure you
earnestly, everyone was perfectly content. The native did
not really mind being flogged for some misdeed. It was
the sort of punishment he understood. Nor did he mind

being uprooted from his family and village and forced to work for six months in another part of the territory. To force an African to work, one is told, is part of the Portuguese process of civilising him. If one points out that less than one per cent of the native population in all Portuguese Africa enjoy any other status than that of uncivilised units of labour, one is told that here again the reason is economic. Portugal lacks the resources to build schools, for example— for literacy has been the first condition an African must comply with to attain the rights of citizenship. But again, one is assured, everybody in Angola was content with his lot until the Congolese and their Communist friends started poisoning the minds of the contented Portuguese African.

Since the outburst in Angola, the Portuguese have been revising their policy towards these territories. The aim is to assimilate a greater number of Africans and bring them into the economic and social structure. But one condition they must accept is that they are Portuguese, not Africans, and even though eventually it is likely that places like Angola may be offered some degree of autonomy, to appease the white settlers, the Angolans must never forget that they are part of Portugal and that Lisbon, not Luanda, is their capital.

This fanatical determination of the Portuguese to hang on in Africa and turn their backs to the winds of change which are blowing all around them, is understandable. The considerations are not only material. To the ordinary Portuguese, these overseas provinces scattered over the globe, are a monument to their splendid past. The word 'empire' may have been erased from their dictionaries, but not from their hearts. It is understandable, too, therefore, that a great many Portuguese are appalled and angered by the attacks in the United Nations on Portugal's 'colonial' policy. The Salazar Government dismisses these as an unwarranted intervention in Portuguese internal affairs. But many ordinary Portuguese feel that the world is 'ganging up' on them in an attempt to destroy the one thing they have left that they can really look to with pride.

Even some of the most bitter opponents of the Salazar
regime are held back by the thought that if the regime falls
the empire might crumble with it.

Before the elections to the National Assembly on 12
November, the Portuguese Opposition had attempted to
issue a manifesto of their aims. One of these was the granting of some form of autonomy for the overseas provinces.
At first the Government forbade its publication, but later
the ban was lifted and publication of this manifesto coin-
cided with a new line in the Government's campaign against
the Opposition candidates. The electorate, grown apathetic
by the realisation that no change can ever be brought about
by votes, were now made to feel that a vote for an Opposition candidate, or even a blank vote, was a vote for the
dismemberment of greater Portugal. This was perhaps
the Government's most effective appeal. (In the end, all
Opposition candidates withdrew, claiming that their campaign had been systematically sabotaged.)

It can be argued that in some parts of Portuguese Africa,
particularly Mozambique, Portuguese rule has maintained
an atmosphere of peace and apparent contentment. Until
Angola blew up in their faces, most Portuguese were completely confident that nothing like the Congo or even the
Mau Mau uprising could ever happen in their part of
Africa. Since Angola, however, the reason for this confidence—the system of their administration—has become
the subject of some of the harshest criticism ever levelled
at a colonial power, and a great many Portuguese bitterly
resent it. Yet very much the same state of affairs exists in
Portugal itself.

The Salazar regime has certainly brought peace to a
country which had been plagued by political turmoil. It
has maintained a tidy economy which deeply impresses
foreign economists. But Portugal impresses a great many
other people. Here there are no strikes, apparently no
social conflicts, and no discrediting political upheavals. In
thirty years the Salazar regime seems to have created a
situation where nothing dramatic or irresponsible could

ever happen. Portuguese newspapers, although officially no longer censored, have acquired a dull uniformity. There is nothing in them to arouse emotion. To look out over Lisbon in the warm autumn sunshine, or over the serene countryside of the Minho, one has the feeling that nothing so harsh even as winter could happen here. But what the Salazar regime has also created is an atmosphere in which, for a great many Portuguese, the clocks seem to have stopped.

A question one inevitably finds oneself asking is, why has a regime of this kind lasted so long, and virtually unchallenged? One reason is that despite its short-sightedness and stubborn resistance to change, it has done a great deal of good for the country. For years before its advent Portugal was in an economic and political mess. The mass of the Portuguese may be suffering a great many hardships; but then they have always done so. Portugal is basically a poor country and it was this poverty of resources which inspired the Portuguese discoverers of the fifteenth and sixteenth centuries to seek riches in the four corners of the earth. This poverty and lack of opportunity at home have always fired the Portuguese to emigrate. Today, however, it is not only this which makes so many Portuguese want to leave home. They feel spiritually stifled.

Dr. Salazar has always run Portugal's finances with the cautious parsimony of a French peasant housewife. His guiding precept has always been that Portugal must live within her means. To him, a balanced budget and an impeccable financial reputation abroad seemed far more important than making any large scale effort to raise standards of living at home, to build more hospitals, for instance, and more schools.

Dr. Salazar exhorts the Portuguese to be patient, to accept hardship, to work harder. This, he maintains, is the inescapable lot of a poor country. As regards politics, his views are even more positive. Politics, he has implied time and time again, are not a pursuit for ordinary people.

Democracy, he warns, can be a dangerous chimera. He is a man who is trying to live and rule by standards which belong to another age. One miracle that he has performed would seem to be that so many Portuguese have continued to accept these standards. Admittedly, Dr. Salazar believes that when words fail, other methods of persuasion are justified. To put it bluntly, one of the strongest pillars of his regime has been a very effective police system.

One sometimes wonders whether Dr. Salazar, in his idealistic ivory tower, fully realises some of the deeds perpetrated in his name or the extent of the smouldering bitterness in Portugal today. Yet this bitterness did explode in 1958. In the presidential elections in that year the Opposition candidate, General Delgado, aroused such a wave of popular emotion that even the blindest supporters of the regime were shaken out of their complacency. General Delgado polled an officially admitted twenty-three per cent of the vote. Dr. Salazar's first reaction, according to persons close to him, was of shock, even grief. But, the election over, he decided that never again would a president be chosen by direct suffrage. In future he would be elected by the National Assembly, in which there are no representatives of the Opposition.

Dr. Salazar never sought power and his fairer critics will concede that the whole purpose of his life in these past thirty years has been to do what he thinks best for his people. The pity is that he still seems to feel that methods and policies which were necessary thirty years ago are still necessary and justified today. His rigid attitude towards Portugal's overseas 'provinces' against the background of a changing Africa would seem to be one of the biggest anachronisms in his thinking.

Since the troubles began in Angola, Portugal has had to build up a security force in her overseas territories which now probably numbers over eighty thousand men. It has been costing her the equivalent of over two hundred thousand pounds a day. Between May and November 1961 it was officially admitted that Portugal's gold and currency reserves had dropped by about £39 million. Note issue jumped from £175 million to £203 million. The 1962 budget provides for greater taxation, drastic cuts in public works at home and even for a possible revision of Portugal's contribution to NATO. It is a budget geared to a new economy imposed by the war in Angola, and possibly new wars elsewhere. The people who will again be expected to accept patiently the cost of Dr. Salazar's inflexible policies, this time over Africa, will be the Portuguese masses. Rich Portuguese will obviously feel the pinch too, but they have two things which the masses lack: reserves to fall back on and, in this issue, a sense of purpose, for they have so much more to lose if, for example, Angola was lost. While they certainly resent any drastic increase in taxation, it is unlikely that their support of the regime will lessen. After all, it is the regime which ensures their existence.

In a sense, the real threat to Dr. Salazar's ideals is the mentality of some of his closest supporters, this influential minority of Portuguese who take the passivity, the sacrifices and the hard work of the masses for granted. Like Dr. Salazar, this class of Portuguese is rigidly conservative, but for different reasons, and they show a sense of materialism which Dr. Salazar has never had. When they speak about 'safeguarding' the Portuguese way of life against the corrosive influences of the twentieth century, it is their way of life they are thinking about, and they have come to count upon the Salazar regime to guarantee an essential basis for this: cheap and docile labour. They are out to preserve this last haven of Victorianism for as long as they can, and to talk to some of them can be a disconcerting experience. It is not that they are short-sighted; quite the contrary. The Salazar regime and the social, or rather economic, structure it has erected, has meant a prosperity which upper-class Portuguese had never enjoyed before. Looking ahead, which they do, they believe that a democratic system of government would spell the end of their way of life.

Portugal is a country of monopolies where a group of
families and their relations and connexions control almost
every worthwhile undertaking in the country and in the
overseas territories. The indifference which some of these
Portuguese show towards the conditions of life of the great
majority of their countrymen is startling. Although real
poverty is all around them, they refer to it in much the
same way as a man in a London pub might remark casually
that there was an outbreak of 'flu in Paraguay.

Many of these privileged Portuguese can read the writing
on the wall, not only in Africa but in Portugal itself. But
all they seem to be doing is to try to stave off a possible
day of reckoning, not prevent it by any constructive
reforms, even of their thinking. They maintain, and far
more bluntly than Dr. Salazar, that the average Portuguese
is not to be trusted with politics. They also argue that
Portugal is an oasis of peace and simplicity in an increasingly materialistic and wicked world; and they point to
events in Angola as proof of what can happen as the
result of 'foreign influences'.

Communism is the nightmare of this class of Portuguese.
They argue that they are fighting it in Africa while the
rest of the world sits back. They also maintain that the
alternative to the sort of regime which Dr. Salazar has
established in Portugal itself could be Communism. In
the political vacuum which they have helped Dr. Salazar
to create, chaos is certainly possible. Yet unconsciously,
in defending the regime, these Portuguese are providing
the biggest indictment of it. In short, they claim that the
Salazar regime has been the best form of government which
Portugal has ever had; yet, they warn, should it disappear,
the Portuguese would promptly embrace Communism. Do
they really believe all this? The answer is that a great
many probably do not. But they have come to derive
comfort from such arguments. It helps them to contem-
plate the poverty of the masses with a certain equanimity.
They will agree that the average Portuguese is poor; but
they argue that at least he is at peace for his mind is not

being cluttered and confused by politics which he could never understand, or with material dreams which in a poor country like Portugal could never be fulfilled.

The Salazar regime has been fortunate in gaining a great deal of international respect and goodwill. Some of it is certainly deserved. But Portugal today has two kinds of friends abroad. There are those who tend to think very much like the Portuguese *élite*. They also admire Portugal for unashamedly holding high the banner of colonialism and for her uncompromising attitude of standing no nonsense from anyone, from 'upstarts in black Africa' to the United Nations. Above all, they too want to see this last haven of Victorianism preserved.

The other friends of Portugal, who are no less sincere, are those who wonder how long ordinary Portuguese will be content with being mute figures in this artificially preserved set piece of Victoriana. They realise the dangers of the political vacuum and the immaturity of political thinking which the regime and its supporters have brought about in Portugal; what they fear is what would happen to Portugal, not just to a minority of Portuguese, if the masses ever did explode.

# THE CASE FOR PORTUGAL

## RONALD WARING

THERE can be no doubt that the Portuguese Government and the Portuguese people, whatever others may think, regard Angola as an integral part of Portugal and for them its incorporation in Portugal is not a legal trick to sugar the pill of colonialism, but is a meaningful reality.

No student of the history of Angola can fail to be impressed by the facts that Portuguese settlers have been living there since 1483, that they arrived even before the present African inhabitants—the Bantu tribes—swept out of central Africa and killed or enslaved most of the Hottentots and Bushmen who originally lived in Angola. The Portuguese were always outnumbered by the Africans in the ratio of thousands to one; frequently they had virtually no soldiers, and at any one time in the past they could have been annihilated by the Africans or driven into the sea. The fact that they were not, in the whole of that long history, is proof enough that their presence in Angola was welcomed by the majority of the Africans who appreciated the benefits to themselves of Portuguese settlement. There is, in fact, ample evidence of this in the treaties of friendship signed by powerful African chiefs with Portuguese authorities, in the trading agreements made between the two races, and indeed in the fact that when the terrorism broke out in March 1961 it remained confined to a

RONALD WARING is London born and is now a British resident in Portugal. He served before and during the war with the King's Royal Rifle Corps and the Royal Hampshire Regiment, resigning his commission after the war owing to ill health. Since then he has travelled extensively in Europe, the Middle East and Africa. He speaks six languages and has written many books and articles on current affairs. In his capacity as instructor at the Portuguese Staff College for the past five years he has had special facilities to travel all over Angola, go out with Portuguese troops on operations and question prisoners of war.

relatively small area in the north of Angola. There was no reason why terrorism should not have spread; the Portuguese were entirely unprepared, there were only 2,000 white troops in a country of half a million square miles (the size of France, Germany, Spain and Portugal put together) and there were barely seven hundred policemen, of whom nearly half were Africans. Thus there was no physical reason why the terrorism should not have spread, yet it did not do so in spite of every effort on the part of the terrorist leaders—using bribery, intimidation, superstition and other means of coercion.

Portugal herself feels intensely bitter about the way in which she has been treated in the United Nations and by those whom she thought were her friends and allies. A completely unprovoked attack was organised outside Angola against a peaceful population. This fact is admitted by the terrorists, who agree that the whole operation was planned in advance in the former Belgian Congo. On 15 March 1961 terrorist gangs struck suddenly at some forty-five different points all over northern Angola. Their attacks were synchronised to take place just before dawn, and in that first day over 300 Europeans were butchered with almost unbelievable savagery. In the three weeks which followed another 1,000 Europeans were murdered together with more than 6,000 loyal Africans. It was the biggest slaughter of Europeans which has taken place in Africa in this century and it passed almost unnoticed in the world Press.

Hemp grows wild all over the Lower Congo, and its extract, hashish, has been used for centuries in religious ceremonies and tribal magic. It was collected by the terrorist leaders and distributed to their gangs. This was done as part of a deliberate plan to loose a horde of drug-maddened primitive savages on a peaceful and unsuspecting community, and the terrorist leaders admit to its being so. The results can hardly be described; women were raped to death and crucified, children burnt alive and others, with their eyes gouged out, left to wander until they died, men and women slowly hacked to pieces or sawn up alive on circular saws. The terrorists in Angola, like the Mau Mau in Kenya, have a religion of their own. It is a parody of Christianity in which the Sacrament of the Host becomes an act of cannibalism. I saw some of these things myself and I will not easily forget them. These tortures could only have been the product of minds of those who, under the influence of drugs, had ceased to bear any resemblance to human beings.

The reaction of the world was strange. The whole Afro-Asian pressure group came into action describing the terrorists as gallant fighters for freedom from Portuguese oppression and colonial ill-treatment. The Communists threw the whole weight of their massive propaganda-machine into the attack; American and some Nonconformist missionaries added their voices, and for various reasons the Governments of Britain, France, America and Portugal's other allies in NATO took up a position of hostile neutrality.

The attack on Portugal in the United Nations is led by Ghana and is supported by Mali, Guinea, Senegal and many others. Sanctions are demanded and it has already been proposed that the United Nations should declare war on Portugal. The object is to drive Portugal from all her overseas Provinces, irrespective of the consequences—and with reason, for Angola is a key point in the over-all plan for the subversion of Africa. In this long-term Communist plan Angola is the gateway to the south and west of Africa. Men like Nkrumah and Sékou Touré have other motives; they see themselves as the black dictators of Africa. The present rulers of the former Belgian Congo also see advantages for themselves, and the Asian countries, which are united only in their basic hatred of the European, can be relied on to rally against any 'colonial' or 'imperialist' power.

Portugal suddenly found herself the accused party; the victim had suddenly become the assassin, evidence in her favour was ignored, and stories, no matter how fantastic, were eagerly accepted as 'incontrovertible proof' against her. Standing in the dock in the United Nations in New York, she is lectured and admonished, insulted and threatened.

One thing is certain, and that is that though Portuguese may die in Angola, they will never willingly leave a country where they have settled for so many centuries and which they feel to be an integral part of their homeland. Many young soldiers to whom I spoke in Angola told me that after the emergency they want to be demobilised in Angola itself. 'This is our country', they said, 'and we want to stay and make our homes here.'

My own view, and I believe that it is shared by many of the British residents in Portugal, is that Portugal has been a little naïve. She seriously believed that in the middle of the twentieth century her allies would support her, even if it did not suit them to do so. She believed in outworn ideas of friendship and decency. She did not realise that British policy depends on the approval of the Afro-Asians in the Commonwealth. She did not appreciate that America, for reasons of trade and for votes in the United Nations, is committed to the continual appeasement of the Afro-Asians, even against the interests of her old allies in Europe. Portugal believed that there were things of greater importance to disturb the councils of the U.N. and that she would be left alone to develop a Luso-African civilisation in Angola. She had done the same thing before in Brazil, and was already in a fair way to evolving it in Angola; in the past thirty years the process has been speeded up enormously. She believed that her policy of racial integration and a Luso-African civilisation in Africa was the best answer to the aspirations of the Africans and the development of the country. It could have been achieved peacefully and without the bloodshed, chaos and misery which has accompanied 'independence' in so many other African countries. The Portuguese were naïve enough to imagine that such considerations as the welfare of the unfortunate inhabitants would carry any weight at all with the theorists, with the Communists and with the African nationalists whose vociferous championing of the African peoples too often conceals nothing other than personal ambitions.

## The British Position

The British Government's attitude towards Portugal's policy in Angola would appear to be influenced by political motives rather than considerations of evidence. The only evidence which the British Government seems to have received on this matter comes from certain missionaries, from reports from the Consul in Luanda, from British parliamentarians and journalists who visited Leopoldville and from the British fact-finding mission which was sent to Angola in July 1961 to enquire into the charges made by the missionaries.

From a detailed examination of the evidence, certain facts are immediately apparent: the evidence of the half-dozen missionaries is not supported by other missionaries who deny certain facts altogether; independent foreigners who were living in northern Angola and who were present at the time when the missionaries state that the Portuguese murdered in cold blood hundreds of thousands of innocent natives, state that to their knowledge this is quite untrue.

Certain journalists who visited the former Belgian Congo, and who claim to have made an illegal entry into Angola, also say that the Portuguese committed many atrocities and their evidence is backed by a number of Labour Members of Parliament, one or two of whom went to the Congo Republic and heard these atrocity stories at first hand from alleged survivors. On the other hand, the British fact-finding mission, consisting of the Military Attaché from Lisbon, the Air Attaché and the British Consul-General in Luanda, was unable to find any evidence whatever in support of the charges made by the missionaries, and they were given facilities to visit the various places where these atrocities were supposed to have taken place. A British Member of Parliament, Mr. John Biggs-Davison, together with an experienced journalist, Commander Martelli, also visited Angola in October and found no evidence in support of the charges. I myself was in Angola at the time and in some of the places where such events were supposed to be happening. I was with Portuguese army units which were supposed to be butchering the innocent inhabitants, and I saw nothing whatever to support these charges. Shortly afterwards, Mr. Richard Beeston of the *Daily Telegraph* passed through all this area and he reported that he had come across no evidence whatever to support the missionaries' charges. Thus, on one side we have the evidence of some half-dozen missionaries, mostly American but some British, and some rather doubtful evidence collected from the Congo by some journalists and one or two Labour Members of Parliament. On the other hand we have the evidence of many other missionaries who say that the alleged atrocities never took place, and they are supported by the on-the-spot evidence of independent foreigners such as the Dutch geologist Doctor H. R. Korpershoek, by the evidence of myself travelling with the Army units, by experienced journalists like Commander Martelli and Mr. Beeston, and also by Mr. Biggs-Davison, M.P., who travelled through the whole area; and finally they are supported by the British fact-finding team sent out by the Government who were unable to find any evidence of Portuguese atrocities.

It would seem that on the evidence available a firm British Government policy against Portugal could hardly be based on the evidence proffered by a few missionaries, as it is completely unsupported by other first hand, reliable sources.

However, the British Government's policy towards Portugal is one of rather hostile neutrality. An embargo on the sale of any arms or war materials whatever to Portugal from Great Britain has been imposed and has already cost the country some £25 million in export orders. Instead of buying from Britain, the Portuguese now buy from Germany, Italy, France and the United States. This

embargo is extended even to cover parachutes for the
dropping of medical supplies. The British consulate in
Lisbon informed some British residents there unofficially
that they did not approve of the organisation of collections
for the Red Cross by British residents, that contributions
towards the purchase of ambulances for Angola was not
encouraged, and that the embassy frowned on the collection of money from members of the British community
which might go towards the comforts of the Portuguese
troops over Christmas. To say that the British Government's attitude is one of strict neutrality is not entirely true.
It is clear that the Government disapproves of Portugal's
action in Angola, and that they will even sacrifice a possible
£25 million worth of exports to mark that disapproval.
When it comes to authorities frowning on contributions
made to the Portuguese Red Cross by British residents in
Lisbon, then it is clear that the attitude of the Government
is more hostile than neutral. The attitude of the British
Government towards Portugal seems to be dictated by two
factors. In the first place, there is the Afro-Asian pressure
group within the Commonwealth; it is clear that since
the United Kingdom is trying to enter the Common
Market, the British Government does not want trouble
with the Afro-Asian members of the Commonwealth,
particularly at such a time. To support the Portuguese in
Angola would strain relations with these members.

The Conservative Government has consistently followed
a certain policy during the last ten years. This has been
to deprive the Labour Party of a coherent policy by putting into effect itself a large part of the Labour programme,
thus leaving Labour only with highly controversial issues
on which they are already split. The Conservative
Government has avoided a head-on clash with Labour.
To support Portugal would unite the Labour Party and
align with them a large proportion of the Liberal vote,
some left-wing elements in the Conservative Party itself,
and bring in behind Labour the vociferous support of the
Afro-Asian countries in the Commonwealth. This would

not only undo the work of years, reverse the whole Government policy towards the Opposition, but it could even bring down the Government itself. Thus, irrespective of evidence from Angola, the Government could not support Portugal in this issue. It has not entirely burnt its boats with Portugal, and has abstained from voting in the United Nations. It is a great pity that the British Government has acted in this way towards Portugal. It has given encouragement to the forces of subversion all over Africa, it has tacitly condoned terrorism—with all its attendant trimmings of murder, rape, torture and arson —it has bewildered the Portuguese who have always looked to Britain for fair play, and it has lost a good friend for Britain without even gaining the goodwill of the Afro-Asians.

## The Terrorists

For the outside world the principal terrorist leader is a man called Roberto Holden. He is reputed to be a good friend of Mrs. Eleanor Roosevelt, and is apparently accepted as a person of some consequence internationally. Recently he attended the Belgrade Congress of the 'neutral' nations, and returned in an official United Nations' aircraft together with the delegation from the Congo Republic. The Portuguese Government protested about this, and the U.N. authorities made the rather lame excuse that they had no idea that he was on their aircraft.

Holden admits to being the leader of UPA (*l'União des Populacões d'Angola*). He is said to be intelligent, very ambitious and an excellent orator. Oddly enough he does not seem to enjoy much authority or popularity amongst the terrorists in Angola itself. Several prisoners told me that they thought that Kasavubu was the leader of the UPA, while the great leader for all of them was Lumumba. The fact that he is dead was not known to any of them, or if it was known, was disbelieved. It would not greatly matter if they did realise Lumumba is dead since for many of the hardcore terrorists he is already a symbol. Most of the terrorists to whom I talked knew of the existence of Holden, but except for some of the men from Leopoldville, the majority were inclined to consider him of very secondary importance. Quite definitely, Holden cannot be considered to have any significant following in Angola, even amongst the terrorists themselves.

There are a number of secondary leaders, and there is evidence that amongst them are European advisers. At least one of these was photographed in Angola with terrorist gangs, and either the same man or another was killed in action with the Portuguese Security Forces shortly afterwards. There is no doubt that amongst the leaders there are specialists in jungle warfare, and for some months past specialist instructors have been training terrorist gangs both in Angola and in the Congo. These men are certainly foreigners, Africans who have received special training in the subversive warfare schools in Prague, and possibly some of them may be Europeans. Holden himself is now under a good deal of criticism, and it is known that there is considerable disagreement amongst the UPA leaders in Leopoldville. He has admitted that his attempt has failed—at least initially. For all its foreign aid, and despite the money received, the arms purchased and the instructors sent to train the terrorist gangs in jungle warfare, UPA has never been a really efficient organisation and its direction has been very largely left in the hands of Africans who are now quarrelling amongst themselves. The M.P.L.A. is a far more dangerous organisation which is now moving to the front.

The M.P.L.A. (the Popular Movement for the Liberation of Angola) is headed by Mario Andrade. It was formed as far back as 1956 and is a purely Communist organisation. Andrade is another Angolan African, but a Party man who has travelled extensively in Red China and Russia. In fact he has only recently returned from Red China where he was promised arms and, if necessary, 'People's Volunteers'. The M.P.L.A. has kept out of

events in Angola to a great extent, and although Andrade
has co-operated with Holden, his policy appears to have
been one of 'wait and see'. It is now clear that the Communists have become exasperated with Holden and his
bungling of the whole affair, and the M.P.L.A. with its
highly trained and specialised personnel and international
Communist direction have now decided to take a hand in
the matter themselves. This is a very serious matter. I
was unable to find any direct evidence in Angola of direct
Communist indoctrination or interference other than the
creation of the People's Socialist Republic of Nambuangongo, which clearly was intended to have a Communist-
type administration, and it seems likely that the Communists deliberately refrained from taking an open part
in the attempt to overthrow the Portuguese administration
and drive the Europeans out of Angola. This is not
unusual, in fact it follows the normal pattern in other
African countries where the Communists have worked
through the slogans of nationalism and independence, and
used nationalist front organisations.

The initial attempt having failed, and UPA having consistently demonstrated its incompetence, it seems likely
that the M.P.L.A. will be forced to come more into the
open. It is known that they have considerable funds at
their disposal, trained personnel, arms, and although
Andrade is the figurehead, the real direction is in the hands
of European Communists. It would not be politic to
publish what is known about this organisation, and at any
rate for the moment Holden and UPA continue to hold
the centre of the stage. They still receive money, still
receive arms, have received some material from America
which I have seen myself, and they are still acclaimed
by the Afro-Asians and the Communists, and also, alas,
by socialists and liberals in Europe and by democrats in
America as the responsible leaders of a movement for
the national independence of Angola.

These are the same men who cheerfully admit to having
organised the terrorism in Angola and, as a matter of

considered policy, to have issued hashish to encourage
their terrorist gangs to commit unheard of brutalities on
an unsuspecting and peaceful population, both black and
white.

## Outside Influences in Angola

In all probability, not a single major leader of the
terrorist movement has been in Angola since the outbreak
of the trouble.   Their headquarters are located in Leopoldville and it was from there that the whole action was
planned.   The first stage was to send a number of
agitators into Angola to make contact with the witch-
doctors and with some chiefs who were thought to be venal
or disloyal.   Possibly not more than thirty or forty
agitators crossed the frontier and made this initial contact.
They promised 'independence', and explained that once
the Europeans were killed or driven out, as had happened
in the Belgian Congo, everything could be shared out
amongst the Africans, that there would be no more
necessity to work, the banks would provide everyone with
money, and a new era would begin.   I was told this by
men who had been contacted by these agitators before the
trouble broke out.   Unfortunately, many believed it.   The
main recruiting agents for the terrorists in Angola itself
seem to have been the witch-doctors, the catechists from
some of the missions (Protestant and Catholic alike) and
some minor local chiefs.   In the towns there were ready
converts amongst the semi-educated Africans who considered that they should have better jobs and more pay.

The second stage was the infiltration of a large number
of 'volunteers' from the former French and Belgian Congos
into Angola and they formed the hardcore of the terrorist
movement.   I spoke to some of them who had been
captured: one, who had served five years with the French
army in Indochina, was typical.   He had been told that
with his great military experience he would immediately
be made a general in the terrorist forces in Angola.

He was thoroughly disillusioned and added (he did not speak Portuguese): *'Je crois que j'etais bien bête'*.

The frontier between Angola and the Congo is immensely long; it consists of over 1,300 miles of mountain, swamp, jungle and elephant grass. The Congo River is full of thickly wooded islands and it is no problem whatever to cross the frontier at virtually any point.

It is difficult to estimate accurately the numbers of 'volunteers' who came in from the Congo but intelligence estimates have put the figure at about 5,000. Once in Angola they were joined by locally recruited men, and when the wave of terrorism started they were joined by very many others who enlisted from fear of the consequences to themselves and their families if they did not. At the height of the trouble there may have been a maximum of 25,000 terrorists in all, or rather less than 0.7 per cent of the total African inhabitants of Angola. Of these certainly a half were unwilling terrorists compelled to join by threats; of the remainder nearly half were foreigners— and less than a quarter of one per cent of the people can hardly be said to have been a great national movement. From the beginning, the terrorists received their orders, and their supplies of arms and ammunition from the Congo. They operated at least three radio sets (two of which have been destroyed) and received orders from a radio station in Leopoldville.

In ever increasing numbers their arms, which consisted in the first place mainly of muzzle loading guns, shot guns and machettes, have been replaced by modern weapons, and they are now quite well armed with machine guns, F.N. automatic rifles, sub-machine guns and grenades. Most of these weapons came originally from the old *Force Publique* in the former Belgian Congo; some which I saw, however, were weapons stolen from or sold by United Nations forces operating in the Congo. The terrorists are paid, and apparently quite well. Cheques made out from Leopoldville banks have been taken from prisoners-of-war and dead bodies. But it is another matter to make definite statements of the sources of this money. It has been suggested that it comes from Communist sources; it has been also suggested that money has been received from Ghana, from various organisations in the United States and even from Britain. There is no proof of any of this and all that can be said with certainty is that the terrorist leaders have considerable funds at their disposal and that these funds come from a source or sources abroad.

Although the terrorists in Angola have been broken up by the armed forces and are now scattered in small, disorganised bands, their morale dwindling rapidly and already deserted by thousands who have voluntarily surrendered, the problem for the future depends entirely on what comes from outside Angola; whether more volunteers from different African countries will infiltrate over this indefensible frontier; what aid in arms and money will be given to re-grouped terrorist forces, and what degree of interference there is from abroad, be it from the United Nations or from the Afro-Asian or Communist countries.

## The Portuguese Future in Angola

There are two aspects of this question, the views of those who joined the terrorists and the views of those who did not.

During the time I spent in Angola I had the opportunity to interview a number of captured prisoners. I was actually present when some of these prisoners were captured in operations; others to whom I spoke had been prisoners for a few days and others again had been swept up as suspects or had been in captivity for several weeks. The reasons which they gave for having become terrorists varied; some said that they had been told to do so by the local witch-doctor, others said that they had joined because they feared the consequences if they did not, and perhaps as many of them said that their reason was that they wanted independence. I questioned them further on this and in different words I got from all of them the same answer. For them independence meant only loot of the white man's possessions, as one of them explained it to me, 'First we must kill all the white men or drive them into the sea, then we take over their houses, their plantations, their women, their cars and their banks. After that we will never need to work again and everybody will have all they could want.' In no case at all, although I questioned perhaps forty prisoners, could I find any realisation of the responsibilities inherent in independence. Some said that there would be no need for a government at all once independence had been achieved and the share-out of the Europeans' possessions had taken place. Others said that this was a matter which they left to their leaders in the Congo. The establishment of a 'People's Socialist Republic' at Nambuangongo during the few weeks in which the terrorists were able to establish a sort of local government in this area gives some indication of the real aims of the leaders.

Although certain reforms were undoubtedly overdue in Angola, I do not believe that this was in any way the reason for the outbreak of terrorism, and the terrorist prisoners to whom I spoke confirmed this view. In the first few days it was pathetically easy to murder the Europeans and dispossess them of their goods. Many of the Africans in this part of northern Angola are still extremely primitive and the chance for plunder seemed too good to be missed. It must be recognised that the average African has not got the Europeans' compulsive urge for work. Work in itself is considered to be neither ennobling nor desirable, and where possible it is to be left to the women. Nor is the African very ambitious if being ambitious entails hard work. The average African in Angola is neither politically conscious nor has he political aspirations, but he is not alone in a desire for more money for less work.

Attempts have been made to make out that the Angolan Africans live in abject poverty, ignorance and under a system of slavery and oppression. This is a lie put about for political motives, and is simply untrue. It is clearly not possible in an article of this type to give many statistics but some are significant:

Africans own over a quarter of all the coffee produced in Angola (worth about £15 million a year). They own the majority of the corn crop, much of the cotton, ground nuts, manioc, and the rest of the agricultural produce of the country. They own great herds of cattle in the south, and have substantial interests in the fishing industry. They own businesses, thousands of valuable plantations, stores and trading posts, and the standard of wages, although extremely low compared with British or American rates, can be favourably compared with many other countries in Africa. The birth-rate is shooting up and some towns have trebled in size over the past ten years. The country before the revolt was moving ahead very rapidly with industrial and agricultural development, while the new hydro-electric dams and communications were opening up new potentials everywhere.

By law there is no racial discrimination of any sort, and an African can occupy any post in the administration or social or industrial life of the country. In fact 45 per cent of all the posts in the administrative services in Angola at the beginning of 1961 were filled by Africans and in many cases Africans had Europeans working under them.

Schools, hospitals and social services are all integrated, and it would be quite unthinkable to have segregation on the buses, in restaurants or elsewhere. The African is accepted without question as the complete equal of the white man in the same social and economic level of life.

The population of the whole Province has risen by some 25 per cent in the last twenty years, and in Luanda it rose from 141,000 inhabitants in 1950 to 250,000 inhabitants in 1960, while traffic through the port of Luanda in imports rose from a value of £630,000 in 1931 to over £22 million in 1956. During the past five years 35,000 houses have been built for African workers and their families;

and these few figures alone will show that the country was developing very rapidly indeed in a general atmosphere of peace and prosperity.

There are 93 regional and sub-regional hospitals, another 80 public health centres with small hospitals attached, 32 maternity centres, 205 first-aid posts, dispensaries, leper colonies, etc. If to these figures are added the 62 hospitals and 600 first-aid posts run by private companies and public utilities, it will be seen that the medical services are far from being as completely deficient as has been alleged.

The fact that there are 2,550 primary schools, 3 colleges for primary teachers, 167 elementary schools, 3 training centres for nurses, 13 commercial schools, 6 industrial schools, 46 secondary schools and 7 grammar schools is a matter which is conveniently forgotten by those who state that there are no educational facilities for Africans in Angola. Admittedly there are still nowhere near enough, but in parts of the country communications are very bad and many of the tribes are nomadic, which makes education difficult. There is no doubt that in the future greater opportunities must be made available for Africans to obtain higher education, and plans for the near future include the opening of a University at Sá de Banderia.

Since the legislation passed in September of 1961 all Angolan natives have become full Portuguese citizens and the 'aboriginal' status has been abolished. In the course of the many thousands of miles which I travelled throughout Angola I asked a number of Africans what nationality they were; nearly all of them replied promptly that they were Portuguese, and barely half a dozen in very remote places in the mountains of the south replied that they were Muilas or Gamos, naming their tribe.

From my own observation, I am convinced that had the terrorism not been fomented from abroad, there would have been no disturbances of any sort in Angola. The people were peaceful and happy, and except for the northern part of the Province they still are. Reforms were

required and were in some cases long overdue; very many
of these have now been passed, and more will follow. Here
again there are dangers. Terrorists who see everything in
the form of unpractical statistics do not realise the dangers
of too rapid detribalisation, the resentment with which many
of the older generation view the education of children who
grow up cleverer than their elders, the problems of establishing schools in remote areas and the difficulties with nomadic
tribes. It all takes time, and those who want to see a new
Africa spring into life in a matter of minutes will not realise
this.

Generally speaking, I think that the Portuguese are certainly meeting the aspirations of the Africans in Angola.
The Portuguese theory of a Luso-African civilisation was
working in Angola and more and more Africans were taking
their places alongside the Europeans in a society without
racial hatred and in which the administrative responsibilities
were shared.

The Portuguese experiment was not to be allowed to
succeed, and while the terrorists were loosed in the north,
the campaign of vilification and lies about Portugal and
Angola is poured out in an endless stream by the Press, the
radio and in the United Nations, as a result of the same
forces which have brought about chaos, civil war, bloodshed
and murder elsewhere in Africa.

# THE CASE AGAINST PORTUGAL

## ANTONIO DE FIGUEIREDO

'. . . even if their cries are not heard by God, they will be heard in the hearts of the just and the compassionate' so, significantly, ends Henry Nevinson's *A Modern Slavery* (1906), an account of the plight of Africans in Angola subjected to forced labour and the rigours of Portuguese colonialism under the Monarchy. The fact that this and other historical eye-witnessed documents on Angola were written in English and are ignored by Portuguese public opinion is no mere accident. Portuguese colonialism is but part of a complex political phenomenon of a country which has only for a brief and troubled period—1910–1926 —known a democracy, and a democracy which even then went only as far as the institutional level e.g. Parliament, and left untouched the structure of Portuguese society which was dominated by the heirs of the feudal lords. Such men were turning into colonialists at the time Nevinson wrote his book, and were investing their fortunes in the neglected African territories, partly because of the loss of Brazil, and partly because they were caught up in the general 'scramble for Africa'. Portuguese colonialism can be said to be an extension of their rule.

The colonialist entrepreneurs owned and controlled the media of information, and there was already a tacit censorship in Portugal on colonial issues. Portuguese colonial

ANTONIO DE FIGUEIREDO is an economist who lived in Portuguese Africa for twelve years and was a member of the Committee representing General Delgado's candidacy to the Portuguese presidency. He was arrested in 1959 and deported to Portugal, then came to London where he now remains in exile. He wrote *Portugal and its Empire: the Truth*, and is now writing a book on Angola for an American publisher. Mr. de Figueiredo is the London representative of General Delgado and is 32.

literature forbears to mention facts such as Nevinson described and gives the impression that if any people had a reason to complain under Portuguese colonialism they were the Portuguese themselves pining for Europe in the course of carrying the burden of the Christian 'civilising mission' into the heart of burning and disease-ridden Africa.

Even during the Republican period 1910–1926, when some liberals reached positions of power and in the process became better acquainted with the consequences of plutocratic rule in Africa, no real attempt could be made to reform Portuguese colonialism since there were the immense problems of home reform which were only complicated by the impact of the First World War and the pressures of reaction inside Portugal itself. When Brito Camacho, a bitterly agnostic and anti-clerical liberal statesman, was appointed High Commissioner for Mozambique he could hardly go any further against the prevailing colonial system than sending such official dispatches as the one addressed to the Governor of the island of San Thomé, in which he says ironically: 'I send you a further shipment of 200 volunteer workers duly tied up'. Brito Camacho, as was to be expected, was dismissed after only one year of office, and met with the treatment which was soon to befall General Norton de Matos, Governor-General of Angola in the twenties, who attempted serious reform, particularly as regards forced labour—the basic and ubiquitous system which makes impossible the pursuit of a genuine policy of co-existence between Portuguese and Africans.

Since the establishment of the dictatorship of Dr. Salazar in 1926, a taboo has been imposed on all discussion of the colonial question. According to the Constitution, all Portuguese possessions are Provinces of a single nation, and the mere suggestion of secession is therefore treasonable. Criticism of colonial administration or policies is banned from the Press and punishable by fines, terms of imprisonment or deportation. Furthermore, the Government's monopoly of information services has done much to mould

Portuguese public opinion to the belief that the occasional rumours of forced labour and administrative corruption and abuses are political inventions inspired by Communists, Protestants and other 'agents of sedition'.

The thirty-three years' duration of this meagre diet of misinformation, coming after centuries of obscurantism and deliberate insularity, makes laughable the notion that the Portuguese ought to know more about Portuguese colonialism than, say, the British or Americans. Even those Portuguese who have written on Portuguese colonialism in a more realistic light can be described as having absorbed from foreign sources the background of their liberal thinking.

The cocoon imposed by Dr. Salazar's regime on Portuguese culture has had in Africa many dramatic consequences. For many Portuguese settlers who had been living in impoverished conditions in Portugal, the exploitation of Africans became a morally acceptable expedient; many of the peasant class—rebels in Portugal—became agents of repression in Africa. In addition to forced labour, the implementation of which would be impossible without the co-operation of thousands of people, there are other widespread forms of cheating the Africans. In the particular areas of northern Angola which were invaded by rebels, and throughout the rural areas, shopkeepers take advantage of the Africans' ignorance of measures and current prices and charge them in some cases twice as much as they would informed, and considerably more prosperous, Europeans. Since most Portuguese do not derive their social ethics from democratic ideologies, the background provided by the Catholic doctrines of resignation and the redeemability of sin is a significant element in the prevailing corruption of Portuguese colonial standards.

Most of the Portuguese intelligentsia have refused to co-operate with the Salazar regime, except in the field of the applied sciences, and even here exceptions are to be found working in universities in France, Brazil, the United

States, Argentina, etc. Nevertheless, so lacking in opportunities are the Portuguese that the regime, in spite of the
absurdities and injustices of the colonial system, has
succeeded in obtaining the services of otherwise far-seeing
and intelligent professional men and technicians. It is in
the field of the social, administrative and economic sciences
that selection has had to be restricted to those who believe
in, or accommodated themselves to, the straitjacket imposed
by the power élite of the *Estado Novo*.

It is difficult to understand how official Portuguese
historians reconcile the idea of 'a civilising mission' with
such historical facts as slavery and the various modified
forms it has taken since its nominal abolition. There are
government-released statistics to show that by 1950—four
centuries after the 'civilising mission' began operations—
less than 1 per cent of Africans in Angola have qualified for
citizenship status in their own country, and that as an
administrative concession and not a right. The fact of
forced labour, which has in one way or another befallen
each average Angola family, should be enough to make
them conclude that the peace and tranquillity prevailing
in Angola can only be an achievement of obscurantism and
repression; this is surely more credible than that it is due
to a masochistic or docile trait of African temperament.
They prefer sporadic manifestations against the administration not to be called nationalist because, they say,
nationalism is essentially a European notion beyond the
grasp of tribal Africans. They call it instead 'nativism'.
But of nativism they might find in the history of Angola
abundant examples.

To take official sociologists next, one finds that most of
their theories on race relations are wishful thinking. The
first striking weakness is the fact that it relies almost
exclusively on the analysis of urban community relations—
and less than 20 per cent of Africans live in towns. Community relations in Portuguese Africa tend to follow the
French pattern rather than that prevailing in British territories and South Africa, and legislation towards citizenship

is, like the French, non-discriminating. However, even in the towns one need only study statistical data and divide professions and income groups on a racial basis to find that the existing social economic barrier is enough to keep a tacit colour bar in effect. In Angola, if at times certain professional groups include both Africans and Europeans it is because the poor Portuguese immigrants have had to compete for the humbler and less well paid jobs. If legislation is non-discriminating on a racial basis it is because the Portuguese content themselves with class discrimination.

This does not necessarily invalidate the fact that the Portuguese upper classes, those who, in non-democratic Portugal, have access to and an influence in, the political kingdom, maintain, at least on a social level, a noticeable coolness towards coloured people. The explanation is that they do not see their position threatened and have not been confronted with the problem of high income Negroes seeking social intercourse with them. In other words, the situation has not yet put to the test their feelings on this issue, at least in the forms it has taken in the United States and the Union of South Africa. In most Western white-dominated multi-racial societies political racism runs parallel and in proportion to the degree of prosperity of the coloured groups, and the position of the race problem in Portuguese Africa corresponds roughly to this general rule.

The social co-existence of Portuguese and Africans on lower strata of Angola society is a pleasant and convenient image, like that evoked by distant Brazil. It is as though the higher strata of the Portuguese secretly did mind if their daughters and sisters married Negroes, but perhaps no more than if they married their poorer cousins and neighbours. The trouble is, however, that 80 per cent of the Angolan Africans do not live in the towns and therefore do not enjoy the supposed delights of community relations. The overwhelming majority of Africans lived scattered throughout the rural districts where they rightly suspect that the administrative officials and the shopkeepers gather in exclusively white parties—admittedly also for reasons other than racial, such as cultural affinities—and that they behave in and out of such gatherings as if they are in fact prejudiced against the black race.

Africans are, indeed, in a semi-tribal state, and the nearest numerical equivalent to an affluent group is that formed by urban Africans who have been turned into unskilled workers, mostly as a result of the six months' training they receive in forced labour jobs. Their ineptitude for equality, partnership or self-government is not due to any collective African biological handicap, as the sociologists imply, but to the *Estado Novo*, which can only present such educational results as those revealed by a literacy rate of 3 per cent. Health and other welfare services for Africans are so poorly financed that Angola has barely one hospital bed for 2,250 Africans and there is only one medical doctor for every three priests. From this it emerges that even revenues from African taxes are often allocated to defence expenditure, which means ultimately that Africans are helping to finance the military and police apparatus which keeps them in suppression.

The average scale of salaries paid to Africans—in the 1- to 2-shillings a day range before taxes—could hardly be an incentive to their voluntarily abandoning their tribal subsistence economy, their homes and families. Therefore the forced labour system, on which the entire economy is based, could only be an evolved form of slavery whereby the individual ownership of the slave is replaced by the collective ownership of the African population by the Administration and the community. This means that most of the accumulation of capital by the Portuguese in Angola is comprised of the unpaid differences between the wages paid for similar work in other territories and those paid to African labourers in Angola. The bulk of the production, transport, distribution, import and export businesses is in the hands of metropolitan companies whose ownership is heavily concentrated in the hands of a small minority. This economic development is hardly related to the interests of the African people or even to the vast majority of Portuguese at home. Indeed, after thirty-three years of a so-called 'economic revolution', the Angolan Africans are still amongst the poorest peoples in Africa, and the Portuguese have the lowest average annual income per head in Europe.

Between 5 and 10 per cent, or between 250,000 to 400,000 Angolan Africans had, before the revolt, taken the radical decision of voluntary exile in the Congo, Northern Rhodesia and South West Africa, and their decision was not determined by any particular propensity for adventure but by the attraction of better wages and social conditions, if not by the fact that this was the only possible way to escape the constant threat of violence on the part of the authorities. In African eyes, the descendants of ancient slavers are always the bosses and the rulers and hardly correspond to the official image of guiding civilising agents.

The drama of Dr. Salazar's regime to date rests in the fact that in attempting to delude the many, the exponents of official dogmas eventually deluded themselves. This self-delusion explains why the Portuguese were so unprepared to meet the revolutionary events which have taken place in Angola in the past two years.

In spite of the constant demands for negotiations on the part of the UPA and M.P.L.A. rebels, to which Governor-General Silva Tavares forebore to reply, some Government Ministers connected with defence dismissed African threats as 'children's panga games'. When, on the nights of the 14, 15 and 16 March 1961, an estimated 60,000 rebels slaughtered 1,200 Portuguese men, women and children and in revolting excesses raped, and mutilated anyone, including children in their cradles, on sight, the military situation in Angola was as follows: military forces totalled 3,000 men; this represented one soldier for every 500 square miles, and one soldier for each 1,967 rebels. To defend the borders of the Congo there was only one soldier for every two and a half miles.

Momentarily, Dr. Salazar, who took over the Ministry of Defence—perhaps to suggest that he had no responsibility for this inconsistent lack of foresight (which, bearing in mind his position as omniscient strong man, is rather ludicrous), seems to have curbed the first impetus of the rebellion. This was achieved at the cost of over 60,000 lives and incalculable misery for both the 100,000 African refugees known to have fled to the Congo, and the families of the 50,000 Portuguese soldiers who had been despatched to Angola. Economic disruption in Angola and the emergency expenditure in the period March–October, 1961, which can be gauged by the sharp decrease of over £35 million or 15 per cent of the hardly saved Portuguese gold reserve, are other consequences of the Angolan conflict for which no one in Portugal has so far been called to account.

Dr. Salazar's belated legislative reforms—the abolition of the *assimilado* system, or forced labour and other practices—are not likely to be found convincing. For one thing, the extension of civil rights to all Africans does not carry them very far under a regime where the Portuguese themselves have almost no political rights. The character of the abolition of forced labour in the cultivation of cash crops for export to Portugal is revealed by the fact that its implementation, according to the Lisbon Press, is not to be extended to Mozambique. Yet Angola produces only 10 per cent of the total production of cotton, the crop most affected by the decree, of that of Mozambique. The decree abolishing specific practices and abuses, such as administrative participation in the recruitment of African labour, is also a good example of the Government's expediency. In the process of listing and forbidding those practices, almost as if it were replying to the criticism long launched by foreign opinion, the Government admits, by implication, that they had in fact existed. Furthermore, the announcement that most of the 50,000 Portuguese soldiers sent to Angola were to remain as settlers, indicates a deliberate policy in Angola, on lines resembling those of Fascist Italy's East African empire, and which was previously carried out by a massive programme of immigration whereby, through land settlement schemes and relaxation of immigration requirements, the population of Angola rose from 40,000 in 1940, to 140,000 in 1955 and over 200,000 in 1960.

Thus there is a race between the Portuguese policy of occupation of Angola on the one hand, and emancipation as formulated by African leaders on the other.

There are two national-scale movements which by their international affiliations are of major political significance. These are the *União das Populacões de Angola* (UPA) and the *Movimento Nacional de Libertacão de Angola*, (M.P.L.A.) which, although operating on a united front, seemed to be ideologically divided according to the two general major trends of political thought in the Afro-Asian bloc. UPA has little or no contact with the Portuguese democratic organisations in exile, which alone are in a position to represent the suppressed opposition to Dr. Salazar. Therefore judgments can only be based on the public statements of its leader, Roberto Holden, which are in the vein of extreme nationalism. The M.P.L.A. can be said to be an essentially Portuguese socialist-minded movement. Like the Portuguese Opposition, it has sometimes been accused, and more often been suspected, of Communist affiliations, a misinterpretation which seems to ignore the fact that Portuguese democratic Opposition is faced with a task of fighting the last bastions of Fascism in the world and that it therefore accepts an alliance with Communists in the same spirit that during the last war Great Britain and the United States accepted an alliance with Russia against the common enemy. Significantly enough, the ideological differences between UPA, which is said to enjoy the sympathy of the United States and the support of British and American liberals, and the M.P.L.A., which represents the Conakry-type of neutralism, are growing, and have apparently reached the point of actual fighting between the rebels of both groups. Such an incident is said to have occurred in the Dembos region of Angola.

The M.P.L.A. leaders, Dr. Agostinho Neto, Ilidio Machado, Mário de Andrade and Viriato Cruz, had already been arrested, together with Portuguese democrats, or were under the eye of the Secret Police, long before they had more favourable conditions in which to engage in a more concrete fight against Dr. Salazar's regime. In contrast with Roberto Holden, Mário de Andrade, M.P.L.A.'s field leader, has subscribed to a programme in which there will be no discrimination against Europeans by Africans in Angola in the future. In point of fact the basic objectives of the M.P.L.A. are almost a duplication of those which the Portuguese Opposition has repeatedly made public in Portugal: the right of self-determination for the people of Angola; political amnesty for all political prisoners; civil liberties, namely the legal right to form political parties and establish solid guarantees for their effective exercise; withdrawal of armed forces and military bases from Angolan territory; a round-table conference between representatives of all political parties in Angola and the Portuguese Government to discuss a peaceful settlement of colonial rule in Angola in the interests of both parties. When Dr. Salazar ignored the rebel leaders' demands, the M.P.L.A. carried out their threats of armed conflict, but it never departed from the spirit of this programme in so far as it would have preferred to achieve the emancipation of Angola by peaceful negotiations. In his latest statement, made in Leopoldville on 30 October 1961, Mário de Andrade, after confirming that the M.P.L.A. meant to carry on the armed struggle in Angola, stated: 'There can be no question of engaging in negotiations with the Portuguese Government as long as the Fascist regime of Dr. Salazar, enemy of the expression of the essential freedoms and of the right to self-determination, is in power. Our fight has already put the regime of Dr. Salazar on the way to the place it naturally belongs—the tomb.'

This programme and imagery underline M.P.L.A.'s just position in the complex game of Portuguese politics, which is deeper than the classical drama of colonialism. As long as the Portuguese, unlike the French and the British, are deprived of democratic rights and institutions and have no means of discussing home, let alone colonial, affairs, and have no say in decisions of national importance and responsibility, Portugal's plight can in no way be compared with that of, for example, France in Algeria—in spite of the surface affinities of the two situations. The Portuguese Opposition has had a long fight for freedom and thus recognises the natural demands of others. During the November electoral campaign it stressed its readiness to grant self-government to Portuguese territories in Africa. It has had, moreover, too bitter experience of totalitarian rule to attempt to apply the same methods to others. The lesson of Dr. Salazar's regime is that those who create a fog can be lost in it.

# THE MAKINGS OF A REVOLT

## CLIFFORD PARSONS

SIX years ago, while on furlough in England, I wrote a brief article entitled *Portugal in Africa,* in which I advanced three reasons why Angola was enjoying relative peace in the disturbed continent. They were the policy of assimilation, the stability of government and the character of the immigrant population—sturdy peasants who were ready to work alongside Africans.

Was this a pipe-dream? Today it looks as though it must have been, yet I still believe that had different policies been followed even at that late stage, the present tragedy might well have been averted. The year 1955 marked also a turning point in relations between the Government and the Bakongo people amongst whom I lived for nearly twenty years. Their paramount chief, the king of Kongo, had died in April. After months of negotiation the clans agreed on who should be his successor. They presented him to the authorities for recognition but he was refused 'because he was an assimilate'. This action, described to me later by a member of the Lisbon Government in the words, 'It was legal but it was not right', was indeed the final breach between the Africans and the Government. Their traditions had been despised, a 'stooge' had been set up as their king, and the path to political progress by constitutional means had been barred. When a few months later many of the leading men in San Salvador were arrested, angry passions were still further aroused: and on my return to Angola in April 1956 I found the whole atmosphere changed. The

THE REV. CLIFFORD PARSONS was a Baptist Missionary in Angola from 1940 to 1959. Since then he has been Africa Secretary to the Baptist Missionary Society in London. He revisited Angola in April 1961.

article written *in absentia,* and still to appear in print, could no longer have been written as it was.

Let us now examine some of the problems peculiar to Portuguese colonialism during and after the Second World War.

Portugal's wartime neutrality may well prove to have been one of her greatest misfortunes. Britain, France and Belgium were at war. Africans and Asians from their colonial territories had fought common battles against oppression in several continents, their merchant sailors had helped bring food to the beleaguered garrison of this island, they had come to share not only the hardships but the hopes and aspirations of the mother countries. All this was denied to the inhabitants of Portugal's overseas empire for whom the war meant for the most part economic paralysis, and political stagnation.

The second consequence of Portugal's neutrality was the lack of any sense of urgency in the Government of the day. It was eight years before Salazar, the doyen of Portuguese economists, introduced his first six-year plan—five years would have savoured too much of the Russian steppes. Meanwhile Britain, France and Belgium had gained a start with their Colonial Welfare and Development Funds. Education and health services were treated as priorities, and, although representative government developed more slowly, by 1953 political activity had germinated in most of their territories. This eight year time-lag at such a point in the history of Africa has been a crippling handicap.

Spain apart, Portugal was unique after the war among the colonial Powers in being a totalitarian state, and as Salazar has said, 'anti-liberal, anti-parliamentarian, anti-democratic'. But the war had been fought precisely against this form of tyranny, and had liberated new thoughts all over the world. Everywhere the same question was being asked, 'What does freedom mean for the colonial territories?' In Portugal alone the question was wholly ignored.

It is worth while examining in more detail four claims made by the Portuguese in defence of their position in Africa.

It is often claimed that in Angola there exists a genuinely non-racial community in which inter-marriage is common. In fact the coloured community in Angola numbered only 26,335 in 1950 of whom 10,729 were under the age of fourteen and 22,560 were unmarried. The Statistical Annual for 1954 reports that 12,534 men celebrated religious marriages in Angola during that year, 725 white, 247 coloured, and 11,562 black. It does not state the racial affiliation of the wives. But for civil marriages, numbering 158, the following breakdown is given:

| | |
|---|---:|
| white man marrying black woman ... | — |
| white man marrying coloured woman ... | 18 |
| white man marrying white woman ... | 113 |
| coloured man marrying black woman ... | 1 |
| coloured man marrying white woman ... | 1 |
| coloured man marrying coloured woman | 15 |
| black man marrying white woman ... | — |
| black man marrying coloured woman ... | 2 |
| black man marrying black woman ... | 8 |

In other words the only statistics available show that 136 out of 158 married within the colour, eighteen white men married coloured women, there were three marriages between black and coloured, one only between a coloured man and a white woman, and none at all between black and white.

Nevertheless many would still agree that the Portuguese are more colour-blind than most, even though (saving for the casual liaisons of white men with black women) intermingling today is in the middle of the spectrum rather than at the limits. But in fact the policy has been one of necessity rather than of conviction, and personal observation goes far to confirm that cohabitation has been occasioned more by the absence of white women from the colonial scene thany anything else. Since pentamidine removed the fear of sleeping sickness the number of white women in the country has increased greatly and, though white men continue to have their *mulheres de necessidade,* the number of first-generation coloured offspring is probably less than it was.

## Colour Blindness

A further complicating factor has been the increasing presence in Angola of educated men from other parts of the empire, notably Goan doctors and Cape Verde administrators. Many of these have shown a deeper understanding of African nationalist aspirations than their European colleagues. It was a Cape Verde Governor at Malange who sought to ease the burden of the compulsory cotton cropping and who was shortly afterwards promoted to a post in Portugal's delegation to the United Nations—a post, however, to which he seems not to have proceeded. It is the presence of these men that gives visitors the impression that Africans and coloured people have a fair opportunity of advancing in social and administrative circles, when in practice very, very few Angolan Africans have attained to positions of responsibility. In 1955 the judge of the northern circuit, Dr. Veiga, was a Cape Verdean of African stock, but not long afterwards he lost his position to be replaced by a European.

The price of advancement for Angolan Africans has generally been their readiness to dissociate themselves from the cause of their less fortunate brethren. This is a problem that does not arise so acutely for Cape Verdeans who own no other culture, or for the Indians of Goa.

## Respect for African Culture

African reaction to what successive Governments in Portugal have referred to as their policy of 'assimilation' is that it is really 'cultural genocide'. It does of course assume the superiority of European culture and is the same kind of policy that English Governments in earlier centuries adopted towards the Welsh language and literature. African languages may only be printed in bilingual editions, thereby practically doubling the cost of production. Vernaculars may be used in education only during the first year of schooling. Government officials, despite the inclusion of Bantu linguistics in the courses of the Colonial School in Lisbon, have shown little desire to continue their study after appointment.

## African Contentment

Despite these serious mistakes and omissions, Portugal still had in 1950 an opportunity to adjust her colonial policies to the changing circumstances of our day. Despite the bitterness created by the contract labour system and the physical sanctions that are its concomitant Africans had not yet glimpsed the possibility of ever being delivered from their near-slavery. Those who comment even today on the happiness of Africans in Angola are praising not the minatory system that overhangs them, but the spirit of a people who long since learned the technique of survival in a totalitarian state. 'You cannot stay sad for four hundred years.'

This is not to say that there have been no instances of good racial relationships between white and black in Angola. Certainly in 1950 the resentments of centuries had not yet crystallised into what might be called a movement for emancipation. There were relatively few Europeans in the country—many of them 'poor whites' whose standard of living was often inferior to that of their African neighbours. Particularly in the south on the Benguela and Huila plateaux the descendants of Madeiran sellers of the last century knew how to live with the local people without evoking resentment. With their wooden ploughs, bare-footed children, and unpretentious living they formed an accepted part of the multi-racial society that governments have so often claimed to be aiming at. In the north the only white people to be found when I arrived in 1940 were government officials, traders (mostly single men), and missionaries. There were few, if any, settlers. There was no sphere in which European and African interests came into violent collision. The African was the primary producer, the trader purchased his goods and sold him his necessities, the missionary preached and taught and healed, the administrator looked to the roads, the poll-tax and the maintenance of law. Since 1950 this superficially harmonious pattern of existence has been disrupted, partly by the new immigration policy and partly by the rise of African nationalism.

The years 1950 to 1960 were decisive in the makings of the Angolan revolt.

## Portuguese Nationalism

The first influence in this decade has been the Portuguese Government's policy of immigration. Prior to the war there were few immigrants, little capital, poor roads, inadequate medical services, no schools, the inertia of a *laissez-faire* attitude that was not at all disturbed to see emigrants go to Brazil, to North America or indeed to the neighbouring Congo. In 1940 there were more Portuguese in Leopoldville and its environs than in the whole of the frontier area of North Angola. The growth of the European population between 1900 and 1950 was slow: 9,000 in 1900; 44,000 in 1940, and 79,000 in 1950. These new immigrants were not of the same mould as those who had been settled for many years in Angola. Many have stayed in the cities where their presence has deprived Africans of positions which might well have been theirs had there been no immigration. Those who have gone into the small towns and rural areas, particularly to the northern coffee bearing regions, have too often coveted the land that was near the roads, whether under cultivation or not, depriving Africans of their traditional holdings and obliging them to seek farming space further and further into the bush. In the granting of concessions, although the law is designed to protect African interests, too often bribery and corruption have turned the course of justice.

The Government has not been unaware of the dangers

of its immigration policy and has experimented not very successfully with what are known as *colonatos*, land settlement areas where European peasants are encouraged to develop in Angola the same kind of subsistence farming to which they have been accustomed in Portugal on a cooperative basis, without recourse to the employment of African labour.

Dr. Adriano Moreira, Minister for the Overseas Provinces, was reported in *The Times* on 29 August 1961 to have announced a policy for *intensive Portuguese settlement* of Angola and Mozambique. Special provincial agencies would be set up to help co-ordinate settling. He hoped that men who had been doing their military service in Africa would settle there. 'We believe it necessary', he added, 'to increase the settlement of *our Africa* [my italics] by European Portuguese who will make their homes there and find in Africa a true continuation of their country.' Earlier still, Dr. Adriano Moreira had, on 18 June, addressed the new Governor-General in these terms, 'You must smash terrorism with all the means at your disposal, showing once again that when we proclaim the Portuguese-ism of the overseas territories it is with the determination to extract and to endure all the consequences of this principle.'

## Aims of the Revolt

There can be no doubt that the aim of the Angolan nationalists is political independence at the earliest possible moment. There are of course emotional reasons why this should be so. Independence spread from Ghana in 1957 to the French territories in 1958, bringing self-government to the Bakongo north of the Congo River. In January 1959 King Baudouin proclaimed Belgium's intention to grant independence to the Congo, a promise fulfilled somewhat precipitately in June 1960. So the second sector of the Bakongo nation attained its freedom, and the aspirations of the Bakongo in Angola, half a million in all—already inflamed by the affairs of their king—were raised

to a new pitch of excitement. The Angola Bakongo, however, were a rural people. There were no large towns,
no industries, and the more ambitious among them had
for forty years been crossing the frontier to seek their
fortune in the commercial and industrial life of the Belgian
Congo. Their natural leaders were already there and it
was entirely understandable that, when the time came to
throw off the yoke, the impulse and the organisation should
come from across the border. Thus UPA was born.

Further south the Kimbundu had been drawn into the
life of Luanda, Malange, Dondo and other townships,
where in private and mission schools many Africans had
progressed beyond the primary level to secondary education, and where opportunities of employment in offices and
factories enabled them to get a slender foothold on the
rock-face of western technological civilisation. Here the
M.P.L.A. had had its birth and had seen its leaders arrested,
maltreated and sentenced to long terms of imprisonment.
Their sudden turning to activism had a very urgent and
immediate purpose in mind: the release of their leaders
from the threat of exile and death. It cannot be doubted
that the story current throughout Angola that the Portuguese Government, having abolished the death penalty,
was in the habit of dropping its political prisoners from
aircraft into the sea, was the goad that on 4 February this
year drove virtually unarmed Africans to the desperate
expedient of trying to break open with their hands the
prisons of Luanda. From that time onward, arms were
made available by the Angola Government to its civilian
population and Africans grew increasingly fearful of a
massacre of those of their leaders who were still at liberty.

But behind these immediate purposes there lay the
memory of long years of exploitation and harsh dealing
that, hidden beneath a patient and polite exterior, smould-
ered steadily. The flow of immigrants increased their fears
of continuing domination by a people whose Government
was dedicated to the task of proving to the world that
'Angola is as much a part of Portugal as is the Minho or

the Algarve'. If anything was to be done, it had to be done quickly.

Both UPA and the M.P.L.A. have their manifestos and in both it is made plain that there is no desire to 'push the white man into the sea'. What the white man must learn, however, is that there can be no privilege based on colour alone, and that any Government must draw its authority from the people on the basis of a broad franchise. How far this purpose remains firm after the experiences of the past few months, it is impossible to say. But one can never forget or underestimate the immense capacity that Africans have revealed for forgiveness.

### Strategy

The strategy of the revolt can only be deduced from events. There is no clear indication of an over-all plan of campaign, and it appears likely that there was little co-ordination between the different bands of guerrillas that went into action on 15 March. The general policy, however, seems to have been to attack isolated farms, commercial settlements and Government outposts, while at the same time disrupting communications by the destruction of bridges and ferries, the felling of trees and the digging of ditch-traps in the roads. In reply the Portuguese withdrew their nationals to the chief centres, evacuating women and children to Luanda or to strongly defended towns like Maquela, Carmona, San Salvador and Ambrizete. The settler community formed itself into vigilante groups and in the early weeks were the hard core of European resistance. They knew the local topography, they were well acclimatised and they had their homes and livelihoods to defend.

It would seem that the strength of the guerrilla organisation was in a swathe of territory from the Congo border, between Luvo and Kimpangu, a distance of about sixty miles, down through Bembe, Nova Caipemba, Mucaba, Nambuangongo and into the mountainous region of the Dembos. The coastal strip was not greatly affected, as it offers little cover for guerrilla fighters. The population is in any case sparse, and the European townships of long standing. Eastward of the battle area, the Zombo people, though as eager for independence as any, were not convinced that military action was necessary. They appear to have believed that negotiation was possible and that with United Nations support they could secure by non-violent means the freedom that they sought.

During the first assaults many European settlers suffered appalling deaths with their families, a terrible and repugnant feature of the uprising that has been well publicised by the Portuguese authorities. No one in his right mind will excuse the murder of innocent women and children and this series of outrages remains a blot upon the insurrection. But it has to be seen in the perspective of years of oppression and cruelty, and not least of the reprisals that have followed. There have been no official figures of those Portuguese who were killed without a chance of defending themselves, but the propaganda of the Government cannot be regarded as reliable. The Annual Report of the Diamond Company of Angola (DIAMANG) dated 30 June 1961 estimated 200 Europeans killed. Since all European women and children must have been withdrawn from the danger zone within a month of the outbreak, say 15 April, this figure, coming into print ten weeks after that date, is I believe significant. How many were women and children? It is very probable that a few incidents have been publicised and re-publicised with the set purpose of exaggerating the element of atrocity.

The strategy that may have lain behind the assaults on outlying settlements was to force Europeans away from those bush and forest areas where Africans could move freely: to clear their flanks, as it were, before assaulting the centres on the roads. In the event this was probably a mistaken policy since by the time they began attacking the major settlements, the many Europeans who had withdrawn there, were inflamed by the reports of outrage on their neighbours and stiffened for militancy. It also gave time for the army to reinforce these places, not infrequently by air. The significance of aircraft in modern military operations, both for transport and combat purposes, had evidently been underestimated by the nationalists.

What provoked them to this action, so patently hopeless in terms of military logistics? There is no single answer, but, in the complex of motives, despair that Portugal's military potential was for ever building up in Angola must rank very high; optimism too that as the Belgians had pulled out of the Congo so the Portuguese would pull out of Angola and naïveté in regard to the effectiveness of guerrilla tactics against the whole panoply of modern warfare. Finally there must have been a strong hope that the United Nations would take some positive action to support them in the essential justice of their cause. The biggest mistake was to underestimate the intensity and ruthlessness of Portuguese counter-measures.

*Atrocity*

The undoubted atrocities perpetrated by some nationalist groups remains in part a mystery.

I can only suggest some considerations that may in part explain what happened. (i) The bitterness of the cruelties endured by so many through the years. The use of corporal punishment, still defended by some in our own country, has no one to question it in Angola. It is a part of life as everyone knows. The cheeky house-boy, the man who omitted to raise his hat to the *chefe de posto,* the clumsy labourer, the chief unable to produce the requisite number of 'volunteers'—all have savoured the *palmatorio* or the *chicote.* Doctors and nurses of our own missions have tended the hands of people beaten in this way. I myself have seen the backs of lads whipped in 1959 for no other reason than the suspicion that they might have been discussing politics. Pregnant women working on the roads have sometimes aborted under the ill-treatment of *cipaios* (African policemen) and girls have known only too well seductions by them and by European officials, with little hope of redress.

(ii) The break-out from servility. For Africans habitu- ated to be servile, who had so often been the recipients of injustice and harsh treatment and for whom a protest meant additional punishment, it must have needed a cataclysmic psychological upheaval to break out from the frame of mind that endures everything, into a new world in which blow is exchanged for blow. One can well imagine that having exchanged one mentality for another, the desire for vengeance must have been overwhelming, and the outward manifestation of a new 'manhood'.

(iii) Drug-taking and holy water. Much has been heard of the besotted and deluded Africans who, deceived by their witch-doctors, hurled themselves to death on the weapons of their adversaries. It need not be doubted that the nationalists in common with soldiers all over the world had morale-boosters in the form of drink, drugs or even 'holy water'—incidentally not a feature of Protestant practice—but you can't have it both ways. If the Africans were drugged and irresponsible, the atrocities, however horrible, lose the opprobium attaching to moral delin- quency. It cannot be questioned that in the two or three years prior to the events of last March there had been a surge of religious atavism in the Bas Congo on both sides of the border.

(iv) The weapons used by the nationalists. The vast majority of fighting men appear to have been armed with little more than knives, matchets and muzzle-loaders. Stories of Ghanaian soldiers and of Czech arms have never been substantiated, and it is probable that the only modern arms possesed by the nationalists were either captured from the Portuguese or acquired during the months of confusion in the Congo. There is no evidence of any provision of arms to the nationalists from outside sources. Combat with knives is necessarily a bloody business and the passions aroused by this kind of in-fighting go far to explain the mutilation of bodies.

(v) The presence of a criminal fringe in any body of fighting men. There will always be bad elements in every army; and the Portuguese forces have proved no exception. Selective reporting however has tried to conceal these atrocities from the Portuguese public.

## Angola and the Churches

Africans have owed their education to religious missions where the emphasis of both Catholic and Protestant has been on obedience to the constituted authority. But neither Catholic nor Protestant would accept that the constituted authority is always right. Both rate loyalty to God above loyalty to man, and on occasion will say so. Many Christians would hold that in 1926 strong authoritarian government was necessary in Portugal itself and the extension of this principle to Angola occasions no surprise for all colonial governments up to 1945 were authoritarian and non-representative. But the year 1950 was crucial: and in the succeeding decade the relationships between the Roman Catholic Church and the regime have grown increasingly strained. The Bishop of Beira in Mozambique has outspokenly criticised the Government's labour policies. The Bishop of Oporto in Portugal itself has had to take refuge in Spain. The hierarchy in Angola has issued a number of strongly worded pastoral letters, *but* (and this is the tragedy) the Church in its highest leadership has chosen not to jeopardise its privileged position by that clear-cut unequivocal denunciation of injustice and repression that would have made its stand so salutary. This is the price of a 'special relationship' which, while avoiding the cachet of 'establishment', has obtained many of the advantages of that status. Protestants in their under-privileged position have worked loyally with the authorities, as countless statements made by governors and inspectors attest, but they have always been accused of foreign-ness and of having a denationalising influence. What has really been under attack has been the Protestant practice of giving the laity (in this case the Africans) a significant part in church government, for any training of Africans for responsibility has been viewed with suspicion. Angola Africans, both Protestant and Catholic have longed and prayed for the opportunity of making their voice heard through constitutional channels, but without effect. In the end counsels of violence have prevailed.

Yet many Africans did not abandon the principle of negotiation and refused to take up arms. Some, it is alleged, were even killed for refusal to join with the rebels. This can be believed, but the extent to which 'intimidation' took place has undoubtedly been exaggerated. No doubt a pacifist African in Angola would be unlikely to be treated more tolerantly than a pacifist in Britain in the Kaiser's war. But some have stood by Christian teaching.

## Portuguese Reprisals

A good deal is made of the statement that Portugal had only 6,000 African and 2,000 European troops in Angola at the time of the uprising. Years of hopelessness on the part of the Africans had bred an attitude of obedience, even on occasion of cheerful obedience, to the powers-that-be. Sullenness itself could be a crime, and there was nothing else to do. Nevertheless one may question the Portuguese figures as they stand. According to *The Times* correspondent, 27 May 1960:

Altogether, probably about 2,000 metropolitan troops have been brought into Angola in the past year or eighteen months, contributing to a total of nearly 20,000 soldiers. Although the majority of these are Africans, the hard core of metropolitan regulars is assisted by some 3,000 or 4,000 Angolan whites, who do their two years' compulsory Portuguese military training in their home territory.

The writer then went on to speak of the modern equipment of these forces, of the naval units patrolling the coastal waters, and the creation of an air arm and new military airfields. The new aircraft with their napalm bombs, rockets and machine-guns were within the year to be used to wreak havoc not only amongst the fighting nationalists but also thousands of non-combatant Africans, men, women and children.

The evidence of atrocities by Portuguese civilians and troops is far too formidable to be denied, and indeed even Portuguese sources have concentrated on making excuses rather than persisting in early denials. It has already been mentioned that some areas were not activist at the beginning of the rebellion. It is certain from the immediate evidence of our missionaries in the Quibocolo area, twenty miles south of Maquela, and in Bembe, between San Salvador and Carmona, that many people were entirely ignorant of the plans for revolt, and were not involved in any way. Yet leading men were immediately arrested, brutally beaten, and in many cases shot summarily. The same was true in the vicinity of Carmona where a British missionary, the Rev. A. A. Patterson who had for years enjoyed friendly relations with the authorities was expelled from the district after it became known that he had heard the testimony of one of his most trusted workers about the particularly brutal execution of a number of his own parishioners. The following day his informant was shot. Above all in Luanda, three weeks after the outbreak of the revolt, I was myself the confidant of those who were witnesses to the nightly murder of innocent Africans in the outer suburbs. At that time there was no fighting within a hundred miles of Luanda, yet wanton killing went on in this way, and even in broad daylight. The educated were again the chief object of attack and the brother of the chauffeur of the British Consul, a male nurse in a Government hospital was one of those dragged from his home and shot. I had opportunities of interviewing high officials of the State and they were fully cognizant of what was taking place. It was clear however that they were not prepared to take the risk of protecting the Luanda Africans lest they should provoke the antagonism of the white community. If this were not enough, the white terror spread to the south, to the Benguela plateau where the 'loyal Bailundos' as the Government describes the Ovimbundu

people have their home. At least fifteen leading men are
known to have died in prison and many others are detained
or are fugitives. In Novo Redondo and Mossamedes it has
been the same story: arrests and disappearances. The claim
that revulsion against Portuguese rule is limited to a few
dissidents in the north is one of the classic understatements
of all time. But in the south hundreds of miles from a
friendly frontier and with no suitable country in which to
take refuge, the Africans are, as a visitor from Angola to
this country has described them, 'sitting ducks'.

Who carried out these reprisals? The Portuguese
Government has sought to excuse what took place by
saying that these were civilians maddened by the atrocities
that Africans had first committed against their own women
and children. Africans do not regard themselves as the
aggressors, but as sufferers under a cruel regime for many
centuries. We have no need to ask again how many
Europeans were atrociously murdered. It is far fewer than
Portugal's advocates would have us believe. Civilians
were the spearhead of Portuguese counter-action, but they
had been armed by the Government and the Government
cannot exonerate itself from responsibility. The radio and
Press fomented race hatred and directed public resentment
against the educated and the Protestant missions. The
refusal by Protestant missionaries of the offer of arms for
their protection was interpreted as proof of their con-
nivance with the nationalists. Allowance must be made
for those Portuguese who had lost those who were dear
to them. I knew personally as friends a number of those
who were cruelly murdered in the first days of the revolt.
But it can never justify the measures taken against Africans
all over the country who, because they were intelligent and
educated, were considered potential leaders.

The report of our own Consul-General and Military and
Air Attachés was stated by Mr. Edward Heath in the
House of Commons (31 July 1961) to indicate that there
had been 'cases of arbitrary and repressive conduct by
civilians and by some members of the police, but he has

reported very favourably on the sense of duty among senior
officials and military commanders whom he met on these
visits.' Independent reports do not bear out the latter part
of this statement. One can understand the embarrassment
of military observers who are confronted with evidence of
breaches of the 'laws of war' by their opposite numbers
in allied countries. There will be a strong desire to 'play
the matter down' and this is what appears to have been
done, in Angola no less than in Algeria.

There have been a number of cases in which African
bodies were decapitated and their heads stuck on poles,
incidents which proved as shocking to some members of
the Portuguese forces as to neutral observers. But there
has been much more than this done to the living, some of
whom have escaped miraculously across the border into the
Congo. And of course there is the bombing and strafing
of refugees by the Portuguese Air Force. The plan to
burn the long grass, that was denied by the British
mission, was first reported by the *Daily Telegraph* correspondent on 3 May 1961 and substantiated by the N.B.C.
documentary *Journey to a War* many months later. That
it was not fully carried through was due largely to ignorance
and impatience, but also to the world-wide outcry against
such a patently indiscriminate plan of campaign.

There are many reliable reports of cruel beatings, the
bayonetting of prisoners, the casting of bound men into
rivers, the bombing of villages, the strafing of refugees, and
the burying of men alive. Portuguese official propaganda
alleges that the terrorists have murdered many of their own
people, but this is denied by the refugees. The nationalists
themselves claim that the Portuguese have taken groups
of Africans out into the bush and shot them there, only to
claim later that they had been shot by rebels. The longer
the delay in admitting the United Nations commission
of enquiry into the country, the harder will it be to verify
just how these men met their death. If the Portuguese
forces are innocent they have most to gain by an immediate
impartial enquiry.

Refugees began fleeing to the Congo within a month of the outbreak of the rebellion and by mid-May it was estimated that there were at least 40,000 across the frontier. Responsibility for relief work was divided between the International Red Cross, Caritas and the Congo Protestant Relief Association, with generous gifts from the Oxford Committee for Famine Relief and other humanitarian agencies. The programme would not have been possible either without the co-operation of the United Nations civilian operation in the Congo. Relief did not concentrate on food and clothes alone. Tents were provided for shelter and hoes distributed to enable the refugees to help themselves and not become a burden upon local villagers. These had indeed given a great deal of generous hospitality when their fellow Bakongo first crossed the border, in many cases eating into their food stores and even their seed reserves. By July 56,000 blankets had been distributed and the number of refugees was estimated as 80,000. But the Portuguese Government began to claim that many African refugees were returning to Angola, a statement referred to by Mr. Edward Heath in the debate in the House of Commons on 5 July. On 1 September however the International Red Cross reported a total of 131,000 *registered* refugees and by 3 October this figure had risen to 141,000. So much for the story that Africans were returning, so much for the story that they were fleeing from the terrorists.

## The Struggle of the Nationalists

Militarily it must appear as though the nationalists have little chance of success in their war against the might of a European power, equipped not only with her own weapons but with the not always intangible benefits of her association with NATO. Those who have read of the experiences of Mr. Gavin Young, or have seen the film documentary *Journey to a War*, must wonder how a military victory could ever be won by such ill-armed and ill-equipped legionaries.

Yet history records many instances of small groups who against all the odds have finally emerged triumphant from an apparently hopeless struggle in the cause of national liberation. This too is a genuine nationalist struggle, and it has the overwhelming support of the Afro-Asian world. What is certain is that it will go on, and that it will finally sap the strength of the Salazar regime and bring freedom not only to Angola's four million Africans but also to some nine million in Portugal itself. With the image of political wisdom and economic stability destroyed, Salazar's power will decline. The cost of the war and its indirect effect on the economy of Portugal have already had serious effects on public opinion, and it cannot be long before others of her overseas provinces come to a similar pitch of militancy.

The nationalists also have their own very real problems. Those of a military and economic nature are patent for all to see. But in addition there are the internal political and ideological tensions that Portugal has already tried so determinedly to exploit. The ex-Belgian Congo has demonstrated very clearly the intensity of tribal feeling that can rupture the unity of a new state, and that can so easily be fomented by skilful propaganda. This has not been lost upon the Portuguese. But the insidiousness of propaganda designed to provoke inter-tribal hostility must not be under-estimated.

Another attempt to split the nationalists is the reiterated claim of the Government that Protestants have fomented the revolt while Roman Catholics have shown themselves loyal and patriotic. This is disproved by the arrest of a number of Roman Catholic priests in Angola, including Manuel das Neves the Vicar-General of Luanda, an able and highly esteemed churchman. In 1960 the Chancellor of the Diocese of Luanda, Joaquim Pinto de Andrade was arrested. In Portugal itself many Roman Catholics have shown themselves hostile to Salazar and his policies. Nevertheless, the radio and newspapers have continued to try and provoke inter-confessional strife, with the purpose of weakening the nationalist cause.

There is also some evidence of attempts to create suspicion between the various nationalist groups, be they tribal like ALIAZO and MLEC, or truly national like M.P.L.A. and UPA. The nationalist leaders although not yet wholly united at the political level, are fully aware of the necessity of a United Front. Portuguese politics have, alas, too often been bedevilled by fissiparousness and the cult of personality, factors that still conspire to perpetuate the present regime in power by weakening the courageous underground opposition.

It cannot be doubted that the political opinions of these untried and in some cases untrained African leaders are susceptible of change. Many of them are pragmatists, others are only now beginning the study of political systems, and facing up to the realities of the science of government. If the Congo disaster has brought no other good, it has awakened an understanding of the complicated nature of modern society. But this does not mean any swerving from the path leading to 'immediate independence'.

*Reconciliation*

Are there any hopes of reconciliation between the present Government of Portugal and the Angolan nationalists? For myself I doubt it. The obduracy of the Salazar regime and its reaction to the events of this spring and summer appear to have made impossible any genuine negotiations. The necessary mutual confidence does not exist. Salazar and his collaborators have said so often and so steadfastly that 'Angola is Portugal' that they can hardly be parties to its amputation.

Were there to come a change of Government in Portugal itself negotiations might be possible, since the new Government could dissociate itself from the crimes and repressive policies of the Salazar regime. Certainly a revolution in Lisbon would create a great change in the climate of African opinion towards Portugal, always provided that the new Government revealed its readiness to negotiate an agreement accepting self-government as the ultimate goal.

Much still hangs on the course of events in Angola itself. If the military campaign continues, bitterness will grow, and Portugal may in the end lose even the benefits of a continuing cultural association with the land that she reached first in 1482.

If relationships between Portugal and Angola become irreparable and Portugal were to withdraw and 'leave the place as she found it', would the United Nations be left with another Congo?

Not necessarily. After all, Angolan Africans are far more homogeneous than the peoples of the Congo. Five tribes constitute nine-tenths of the whole population, the Bakongo 500,000, the Kinbundu 1,000,000, the Ovimbundu 1,500,000, the Lunda 400,000, the Ganguela 400,000. The first two have been actively engaged, militarily, in the revolt. The Ovimbundu undoubtedly sympathise with the demand for independence but their geographical situation places them in an impossible position from the point of view of active insurrection. All these are savannah peoples, and their languages and cultures are closely related. Secondly, the Portuguese presence has been a unifying factor. The use of Portuguese as a first language in school has created a medium of communication that was denied to the Congolese where primary education until quite recently was wholly in the vernaculars. The long association of Portugal with the littoral, though not the interior, has meant a certain cultural infiltration that has helped reinforce that greater homogeneity found among the tribes of Angola. Though more Congolese than Angolans have been educated in primary schools: there are more African graduates in Angola than in the Congo. In Angola in 1958 there were twenty-three, a pathetically small number, but one that compares well with Congo's eighteen in 1960: and the eighty-one students now scattered over Europe should not be forgotten.

It must not be assumed that all hope of reconciliation has been abandoned. But if the Government of Portugal maintains its present intransigence, no one should assume that there is no way out of the impasse, that the United

Nations cannot accept any further burden, and that a situation which cries out to the world for remedy must be left to inflame still further the racial passions that threaten the peace not only of Africa but of the world.

# A CATHOLIC VIEW

## HUGH KAY

NO assessment of Portugal's stewardship in Africa can be justly made without reference to her own history. It is, perhaps, a measure of Dr. Salazar's achievement that so many people have forgotten how bad a state his country was in when he took over the effective leadership thirty-four years ago. To this day, what is humanely ordained in Lisbon does not necessarily run in the bush. The reasons behind this account for the whole problem of Portuguese backwardness at home and abroad. There had been no such thing as metropolitan Portugal until Salazar, about twelve years ago, formulated the tradition of centuries into the principle whereby the overseas territories are given the status not of colonies, but of integration with Portugal herself. Goa, the Portuguese enclave in India, and the African possessions formed an extension of Portuguese soil overseas. Salazar's hopes for the overseas territories were bound to take a long time to work out. When he first came to power, he found no competent body of civil servants with a sound tradition of leadership, no aristocratic tradition of unpaid service, no 'kindergarten' of trained administrators to put his principles into effect. His failure though not, perhaps, his fault, is that the education of a sound administrative cadre was still on its way to maturity. The problem was the same at home. Portugal had never enjoyed a stable monarchy since the days of Henry the Navigator. In the twentieth century there were a succession of revolutions, republics, and three-monthly assassinations. There

HUGH KAY is Assistant Editor of the *Catholic Herald*; Editor of the *Glasgow Observer* and *Scottish Catholic Herald*. He specialises in political and industrial reporting and commentary, and has contributed articles for numerous publications. In August 1961 he visited Angola, and was the second British correspondent to be allowed in after the bar was put up early in the uprising.

are those alive who remember seeing an entire Government blown up in a wagonnette on its way back from the funeral of a murdered President.

In the first decade of the century religion was stamped out. Its stabilising power had small chance when only three religious houses, including the English College, remained viable and British warships had to move in to protect Irish nuns. It is only a few years since you could by law shoot any Jesuit on sight with impunity. Many of the modern settlers in Portuguese Africa derive from this generation of unbelief and anarchy, which helps to explain the excesses of violence, the denial of human rights, the evils of the labour system—all condemned by Portuguese law but all too difficult to enforce without a tradition among the settlers themselves. Moreover, it is only in recent years that there has been a soundly operating Oversea Ministry in Lisbon. Time and again, Portugal herself has been denuded of her most dynamic personnel. It was true in the days when the Jesuits were building their co-operative movements in Portuguese Brazil, in the days when Wellington and Beresford went to the Peninsula only to find a mere 'second eleven' to deal with in Portugal because the cream of the aristocracy had been shipped off by the French to fight the Russians; and so on to the present time. Links with the 'colonies' were, until Salazar's time, slender and slack. The overseas territories worked to their own budgets, developed their own defence plans with hopelessly inefficient armies. Few profits, in pre-Salazar days, found their way back to the mother country. The colonies have been the home, too, of angry masonic exiles, and, like Portugal herself, the victims of an anti-clericalism dating from Pombal's quarrel with the Society of Jesus, coupled with a Voltairean liberalism blown south from the French Revolution.

The Portuguese Communist Party boasts little in the way of strong 'front men', but the 'submarines' are powerful and thoroughly well organised. One of the dangers of movements involving men like Delgado and Galvão is that, even at their best, they stand little chance of success unless they are taken over by the Communists—the only revolutionaries with the real know-how.

After the centuries of discovery—the days of Portuguese greatness—came the centuries of decadence. And then came Salazar, to govern a people with a vast inferiority complex, longing to be taken seriously, longing to get back some sense of national pride and hating the truth that their army was the laughing stock of the European embassies. Salazar's weaknesses, failures and faults cannot obliterate his achievements in restoring stability to a degraded and divided nation. He has trained a modern army and brought Portugal into the NATO alliance. He has begun to integrate the defence structures of the overseas territories. He restored the currency. He came to terms with the Holy See.

One of the strangest effects of the *Santa Maria* incident at the beginning of 1961 and of the anti-Portuguese strictures in the U.N. councils, is that many of Salazar's sternest critics have drawn closer to him. This is not an expression of personal regard. But however conscious the people may be of Salazar's inadequacies, they shrink from what might arise to replace him from the welter of nationalist, liberal and Communist forces competing in the nation's underbelly.

The huge settlements of new flats for the workers in Lisbon testify to the war Salazar has been waging on the poverty of the masses. A network of roads and power stations has sprung up in an agricultural country almost bare of any natural resources—where, in the Alentejo, crops are produced only once in four years because there is no water and irrigation developments are inevitably costly and slow. It has not been easy to derive a viable economy from a country whose main assets are sardines, cork, pineapples, wine and olives. The one real money-maker Portugal has ever had is its natural supply of wolfram, a material in huge demand for armaments, which Britain bought in great quantities to prevent Hitler from getting hold of it.

Until 1950, half the energy of the army officer was dissipated in making sure that his recruits were taught to read and write. It is a sizeable feather in Salazar's cap that somewhere between a third and a half of the population are no longer wholly illiterate. Many new industries have sprung up. Wages are rising. Yet it remains true that such wealth as does exist still tends to be channelled into very few pockets. The day of the 'eleven families' is not yet done. A certain distrust of enthusiasm makes the task of the reformer particularly difficult; the Portuguese seems to fluctuate between a declaration of *parce mal* (bad form) when a fellow countryman shows a little exuberance, and *tem graca* ('how charmingly quaint') when he detects a little energy in a foreigner. But if butter is short it is because more people are eating it. If political opponents are imprisoned without trial, it is because of an obsessive dread that Portugal might slip back into anarchy. And, whatever the inherent values of the democratic method, it must surely be accepted that Portugal's only attempt at Liberal democracy plunged her into a period of corruption, disintegration and bankruptcy—both material and spiritual.

Within limits, Portugal has become a modern country, and development programmes for the oversea territories have made considerable progress. Vocations to the priesthood are increasing; young men are appearing at the communion rail and, in some working-class districts, churches are full. Curious agnostics and anti-clericals have visited Fatima in large numbers, only to return to a practise of the faith. Salazar's failure, if not altogether his fault, is that he has never succeeded in building up an opposition *à la turque,* a controlled body of intelligent criticism, a Christian Democrat movement derived from the superb intellectual tradition enshrined for centuries in the University of Coimbra.

## Colonial Method

Portugal's methods in her oversea territories are misunderstood in Europe. While the British colonial system

seeks to emancipate collectively, the Portuguese prefer to
bring the indigenous peoples to adulthood individually.
In Portuguese eyes it would be criminal folly to leave the
quarrelsome tribes of Portuguese Africa to democratise
their own country under imported European or American
forms of administration which would never take root. The
result of Belgium's departure from the Congo, in the mind
of Lisbon, is a classic example of what could happen in
Angola. The conduct of the U.N. expedition is seen as
precisely the sort of thing feared by Dr. Salazar when he
condemns what he calls 'international colonialism', by
which he means a system that is irresponsible and thus
inhuman because there is no king, no president, no single
national legislature to stand in the dock if anything goes
wrong. The Portuguese does not seek to perfect Africanism
as such. Rather, he prefers to educate the Africans
individually for assimilation into the Portuguese character
and culture. In the field of missionary endeavour, this can
be criticised as being at variance with the Catholic Church's
policy of baptising what is best in indigenous cultures and
traditions, and 'accommodating' herself, within the limits
of defined dogma, to native characters, needs and aspirations. But in the political and social fields, Portugal has a
strong case to argue for her system, and it is a case which
ought to be heard. The whole set-up must be understood
against the background of the multi-racial ideal, the sense
of missionary purpose, the complete absence of colour bar
sense among the Portuguese. The principle of 'Portugal
overseas' is seen as a direct negation of colonialism. It is
for this very reason that the African was to be 'assimilated',
and that, since he was ultimately to 'become Portuguese'
with a share in the administration not merely of his own
country but of the whole of Portugal in Europe and elsewhere, assimilation had to be made dependent on his reaching a certain degree of educational fitness. Even in
metropolitan Portugal, the vote is denied to a third of the
population on grounds of illiteracy.

## The Church's Attitude

Statements of the Portuguese bishops in Africa are not easy to come by. One bishop has had his pastoral letters suppressed by the civil authorities. The fact is, however, that, far from being tied to Lisbon's apron strings, the Portuguese hierarchy in Angola and Mozambique has openly and consistently defended the African people's rights and aspirations even when these seem to run counter to Lisbon's declared policy. The principle that assimilation demands co-operation between governmental and missionary techniques is reflected in the 1940 Missionary Agreement concluded between Portugal and the Holy See. This has always been honourable in intent. But the bishops on the spot are well aware that it can be very difficult to apply in the climate of rising African nationalism, and that it lays itself open to local abuses which Lisbon is too often powerless to control. As a follow-on from the old 'patronage' system, the Portuguese missions are not directly subject to the Sacred Congregation *de Propaganda Fide* (which governs the missionary world from Rome), but to their national dioceses and to the State of Portugal. Under the Missionary Agreement, all missionaries must be Portuguese, except where serious shortage compels others to be brought in. All the bishops are Portuguese-born, except two who are Goans but who qualify for Portuguese nationality under the assimilation principle. Bishops must send periodical reports to provincial Governors. Schools for Africans must conduct lessons in Portuguese. God and Empire are so closely linked in this colonial theory that African languages tend to be stifled, indigenous cultures ignored, and the African somewhat depersonalised.

The 1959 Rome Congress of African Writers and Artists declared that the devoted work of the Church is being diverted by the civil authorities to imperialist ends, and that the Church authorities expressed themselves scandalised by the 1955–56 lists which showed that, out of 4,000,000 Africans served in theory by 911 educational

establishments, only 39,000 were actually pupils. Unable
to be himself, too immature to become wholly Portuguese,
the African can thus easily become fodder for servile functions. Into this picture comes a champion like Bishop
de Resende, of Beira in Mozambique, whose championing
of African rights rings with the language one associates with
Archbishop Hurley of Durban or the Portuguese Bishop
Gomes of Oporto, now in exile in Spain after his clashes
with the Lisbon Government. Distribution of Monseigneur
de Resende's pastoral letters has been forbidden for some
years. In them, and in other pronouncements, he has
emerged as the advocate of a Portuguese University of
Africa, which, he says, should be created in a manner
corresponding to the native people's aspirations. Such a
University, he wrote in one of his pastorals, would 'fuse
the culture of Christianity in its most universal elements
with all the manifestations of local cultures.' It would
seek to capture, develop and orientate all that is positive in
the African mind and tradition. This principle was
accepted by the first Conference of the Portuguese African
hierarchy, held at Lourenço Marques in November 1957.

The abuses of forced labour came in for some biting
criticism from Monseigneur de Resende in a pastoral letter
written in 1953 in which he said:

If you force native workers to live more than six months away
from their families, you are asking for an uprising of the
masses of the people, and the complete ruin of their family
life. Does Portugal really want to lead all the peoples
entrusted to her to a total participation in Christian civilisation
or not? If the answer is yes, as would appear in the light of
our past history, how can it be done without the open and
specific protection of the family? Labour must be safe-
guarded as a matter of free choice, so that the spectre of
forced labour may be banished for good.

And the 1957 Bishops' Conference issued a statement which
declared:

Justice, charity, the dignity of work and the full development of all the territories demands that equal opportunities

of improvement and promotion must be guaranteed for all, without any discrimination other than that based on professional and moral qualifications.

Declaring that it is indefensible for the 'haves' to live on the work of the 'have-nots', the bishops added that under no pretext whatsoever can anyone be constrained to abandon family, home, village and property except in the case of grave public crisis, and only for as long as the crisis lasts. The Bishop of Malanje, in 1959, gave an interview in which he referred to those white people, Portuguese and otherwise, who are trying to 'get rich quick', and whom it does not suit to have black people on the same footing as themselves. Granted this equality, said the bishop, it would no longer be possible for white people to exploit the Africans' ignorance. While not specifically objecting to the Portuguese integration and assimilation principle as such, the bishops of Angola issued a statement in April 1961 insisting that the authorities take into account the just and legitimate aspirations of the Africans, and denouncing ideologies and practices attenuating human rights.

## The Angola Uprising

It is against such a background that the Angola uprising of 1961 must be viewed. My visit there, as the second British journalist to be allowed in since the outbreak of the terrorism, resulted in the publication of a series of articles which, while criticising the Portuguese administration for the errors and faults of past and present, nevertheless presented the side of the story that no one else seemed to want to tell. Baptist missionaries condemned the Portuguese Army for horrible reprisals against the insurgents, and dragged in the dust every detail and aspect of Portuguese influence in Africa. I found overwhelming evidence to clear the good name of the Portuguese Army, and, side by side with the failures, I found evidence of great achievements over the years. My articles were hailed with vituperation from Catholic sources, for the British Catholic these days too often bends over backwards to make himself acceptable to the society of angry young men who feel without thinking, who operate in terms of prejudice and not of judgement, who disregard fact when it tends to be 'unfashionable'. Approval came, on the other hand, from British non-Catholics who are or have been resident in Portugal and Portuguese Africa. My findings have been confirmed by the British Consul-General in Luanda, whose verdict, though given to the House of Commons, received scant attention from the 'liberal' newspapers and reviews which had blindly committed themselves to an anti-Portuguese hate campaign. Further confirmation has come from former British officers who have lived and travelled in Angola (and very few British people have done this). I refer especially to men like Col. Ronald Waring who was personally present at the centre of the fighting, of Col. McKeown, whose series in the *Scotsman* wholly vindicated my position, of several British Members of Parliament, who have made special tours of inspection in Angola since the autumn, notably Mr. John Biggs-Davison, M.P. A balanced view has also been taken consistently by the *Daily Telegraph,* whose correspondent, Mr. Richard Beeston, preceded me into Angola in the summer.

The plain fact of the matter is that between March and June 1961 when the Portuguese Army, according to the Baptists, was waging a campaign of genocide, the total number of Portuguese troops in the entire area of Angola (several times the size of Britain) was well under 2,000. The uprising which, according to the anti-Salazarists, represented a spontaneous outburst of a depressed African nation, in fact involved less than three-quarters of one per cent of the entire African population. Just before the uprising, this 'ruthlessly oppressed' people, 4,000,000 strong, were controlled by a ridiculously small force of police and troops amounting in all to 8,000, of whom 5,000 were Africans. It is a source of real astonishment to me that the Baptists, who have been in Angola for over eighty years, never put up a word of public protest until the uprising in 1961. They could have spoken freely.

The old alliance and general considerations of diplomacy were there to protect any British missionary. The people most likely to be smacked down were the Portuguese Catholic bishops, who, as we have seen already, can be severely disciplined by the Lisbon Government, if it thinks fit, without reprisals. Yet these bishops have consistently criticised the Government for many years before the 1961 insurrection. I am not concerned to accuse the Baptists of dishonesty. But I do think that, in the words of one of their own number, 'my brethren have tended to exaggerate one set of circumstances at the expense of the whole picture'. Before setting down my own account of the Angola story, let me quote a few words of the report made by the British Consul-General in Luanda, after a fact-finding mission for the British Government:

I believe that the majority of the crimes committed by the Portuguese were the work of armed civilians, and that, far from condoning them, the authorities did their best to stop them. In the earlier stages they were, however, prevented from taking effective action to that end, partly from lack of sufficient police and troops, and partly from fear of precipitating clashes between the white population and the security forces.

With the arrivals of reinforcements from Portugal, the situation has greatly improved, and there is little doubt that the army is having a good influence. . . . There is also a good deal of evidence that a large number of Africans have been and continue to be killed by rebels for refusing to join forces with them and for protecting their European masters' lives, families and property.

It will be seen that the settlers who committed atrocities can at least claim to have been given terrible provocation. This does not excuse. It is, however, a mitigating factor. There are the weaker brethren among them, as in any nation, but the missionaries themselves claim that over the years they have been able to make private demands to Portuguese officials for the correction of abuses, and, they frankly admit, these demands have been complied with again and again.

## The Rebel Movements

Who are the rebel leaders in Portuguese Africa? The propaganda of the Eastern bloc in 1961 was turned on full blast against Portugal. States who operate terror as the political norm in their own regimes have been accusing Portugal of a bloody campaign of mass extermination. Radio stations in Iron Curtain countries have been sending out whole series of inflammatory broadcasts to the Portuguese African territories. The campaign began in 1959 when the position in the Congo was becoming less and less favourable to the Communist Powers. The Soviet Ambassador in Conakry, Guinea, is Mr. Solod, a crack operator. He is believed to be in close touch with the M.P.L.A., whose leaders are Communist sympathisers, and some of whom have visited Moscow and Peking. But the leadership of the terrorist uprising in Angola is situated over the Congo border in Leopoldville. The leader is Roberto Holden. He is a Marxist trained in the Congo. His associates are known from the meetings of Communist front organisations. Then there is the Students' Association of Portuguese African colonies, whose headquarters are in Eastern Germany. All the organisations are believed to be financed from abroad, and to have connexions with the Afro-Asian Council's Solidarity Fund, administered by the Chinese Communist Chu Tzu-chi.

## My Visit to Angola

I went to Angola in August 1961. I found enough to complain about. But the image, projected by British Press and television and the reports of Baptist missionaries, of an enslaved Angola, its aspirations brutally and contemptuously repressed by a genocidal army, bears little relation to the situation as I found it. Far too much reporting in this country has come from Leopoldville. The first wave of American journalists who came hard on my heels to cover the visit of the U.S. Assistant Secretary of State, Mr. Mennen Williams, found themselves reaching conclusions similar to my own. It is ironical and symbolic that I returned to Lisbon in company with an injured suspect terrorist, paralysed from the waist down, who was being flown 4,000 miles by his 'oppressors' for treatment too specialised for the local hospitals. It was much of a piece with many things that I saw inside Angola.

In addition to what I saw of the conduct of the army, of Angola's economic and administrative improvements, and of the practice of the multi-racial theory, I sought the testimony of a wide range of local diplomats, journalists, business men and missionaries. Among them were Dutchmen, Danes, Americans, Italians and Britons—Catholic and non-Catholic—not to mention Portuguese settlers and administrators. I had long and very frank talks with senior Government officials whom I found to be surprisingly candid, willing to admit mistakes and seriously anxious to profit by them. Some of my principal impressions may be summarised thus:

The material circumstances of the Angolan African, taken as a whole, are no worse than in comparable territories elsewhere in the African continent—in some respects they are better. The major complaint is that few Africans have received a proper education. The uprising had little to do with popular movements or spontaneous nationalist combustion. It was launched, after long and careful planning, by anti-Salazar Marxists under Roberto Holden in Leopoldville. Recruits were obtained by the traditional Communist tactic of sending leaders into African villages, killing and mutilating a number of men *pour encourager les autres,* and threatening the remainder of the men with like treatment if they did not join the terrorist advance. Wholesale use has been made of the influence of witch-doctors, fetishism, and residuary cannibalism.

Inflamed by the unspeakable atrocities perpetrated by African rebels against white and black alike (I have seen heaps of unprintable pictures to prove it), Portuguese and other European settlers at first went mad and killed Africans indiscriminately. They were restrained by the arrival of the army, which has operated according to the

ethics of legitimate war. Allegations that troops set out
to burn 50,000 natives in the grasslands are absurd to anyone who knows the area and the extreme difficulty of burning that kind of grass on a sufficient scale to ensure the
destruction of large numbers of Africans more familiar
with the grasslands than any European.

The Angolan economy is expanding rapidly. Substantial
foreign investment is coming in to supplement Portuguese
enterprise. The agricultural co-operative villages are proving highly successful. The concept of the soldier-colonist,
whereby the retired army man settles down in the oversea
province where he has served will improve the quality of
the settler community. In spite of its many limitations the
multi-racial principle is not a complete myth. White and
black men may be seen toiling side by side in the same
skilled and unskilled work, sometimes under a black over-
seer.

American missionaries of various sects must bear a share
of responsibility for inflaming unbridled ambitions for
independence in untutored minds. On the Catholic side, the
seven black priests, including the Vicar-General of Luanda
now under arrest, were undoubtedly also involved in the
uprising. But the Catholic clergy have on the whole
remained detached and have openly condemned unlawful
violence on both sides. They have stuck to their posts in
the troubled areas, and two Capuchins have been murdered.
Attendance at Mass has increased since the uprising began.
It is fair, incidentally, to point out that while Catholic
priests number 450 in Angola, the authorities have permitted as many as 300 non-Catholic missionaries to work
in the country.

The Portuguese failure has been in seeking to impose a
disembodied metaphysical principle on primitive peoples
whom it has not educated.

But it may be argued that, while the European policy of
withdrawal from Africa has yielded highly ambiguous
results in the Congo, Ghana, Kenya, and some of the former
French territories, there is a good deal to be said for the

sense of mission and the fundamental staying power of the Portuguese which interplay with less lofty motives in their determination to stand firm.

## The Twisted Cross

One English correspondent, writing in a Sunday newspaper from rebel territory, told me that he had seen the remains of a U.S. fire bomb in a village destroyed by Portuguese troops. It seems, however, that the population of 200 escaped unhurt. It was almost in an aside that he admitted that the village was a terrorist headquarters. His story is typical of those who seem unwilling to concede to the Portuguese army the right to use anti-guerilla tactics. Had he penetrated a little farther into Angola, he would have heard white settlers complaining that, in fact, the army is failing to get 'stuck into' the rebels. And he would have heard the reason why—which is that the army's orders are to reclaim the native peoples, to hold fire wherever possible, and to persuade natives who have been the worst victims of the terror to snap out of the stupor induced by a mixture of perverted Christianity and witchcraft. Catholic and Protestant African catechists have been used by Holden's invading ringleaders to work up natives into a synthetic ferment of anti-white hatred which peters out as the army drives the terrorists back, and the bewildered natives rush to the Portuguese troops for protection. Their technique is to confuse fetishist and Christian symbols: terrorists show a predilection for crucifying their victims. Crosses were traced on the foreheads of natives when they were initiated into terrorist action by men who knew how to exploit their deeper attachments. Terrorists now in Angolan prisons tell you how their tribal witch-doctors gave them drugged potions, whipped them into frenzy, and promised that the white man's bullets could not touch them. Army officers speak sadly of natives dancing up to the firing line crying 'white men's bullets are only water', and then, with the bullets in their stomachs, changing their cry from 'water' to 'hot water' as they died. The language of the Protestant

Bible and of the more stirring marching hymns were strongly marked in directives sent out from Leopoldville to terrorist leaders, and hymns themselves were adapted to rebel themes. Natives were told that if they died fighting they would rise again in three days. As many as forty-two catechists were found among a nest of terrorists preparing to launch an attack on Vilt Vicosa de Seles. They were connected with organisations which subsidise journeys of Angolans to Ghana, Guinea, Ethiopia and the United States. Throughout the whole of the fighting area Protestant missions were untouched. Catholic missions were frequently attacked and two priests murdered. I am not attacking non-Catholic missionaries as such. The behaviour of many Catholic catechists has been shameful. But thinking Protestants in Angola will tell you of their regrets that in their dealings with people who are still quite primitive they have laid so much stress on African independence.

Of all the charges levelled against Portuguese troops, I know of roughly half a dozen only in which place names have been specified in the European Press. One of these is Quibocolo, where, so certain newspapers told us, 500 Africans were mown down by the army. In fact, a young Dutch geologist living and working there at all material times assured me that no such incident has taken place, nor anything remotely resembling it. One may be forgiven for asking where these stories came from. Army officers freely admitted to me that villages had been fired. There is no other way when troops are being shot at by terrorists in places of concealment in a village, and the roads are expertly ambushed by felled trees and camouflaged pits in what has been described as a highly sophisticated and well planned operation. The British Consul-General, who had toured the troubled areas, told me that he had heard rumours of army excesses but had never encountered an eyewitness.

It was at Caxito that I saw something of the social psychology schemes of the army. As the troops moved up, they set up schools and welfare centres for helping the native communities back to normal. I met Captain Ruy Mendoza, a young man who was the talk of the territory, who fits naturally into the traditional role of the Portuguese army officer and N.C.O. as educator. It was a strange sight to see Mendoza and his men surrounded by little black children learning from illustrated primers and making their wooden models with an astonishing display of imagination and skill. Just down the road, at one of the plantation hospitals, now taken over for the army, I saw suspected terrorists lying side by side with young white soldiers—all receiving the same surgical and medical treatment.

The reason why the Portuguese, unlike the British, refuse to leave Africa is precisely because of their centuries-old belief in their unique capacity for multi-racial partnership. This is not a myth. It is obvious the moment you enter Lisbon. There is Africa on the street and in the architecture, in the features of its people, in its acceptance of inter-marriage. It is a city where 'half-caste' is not an insult but a simple statement of fact. Ethnically, Portugal is the natural link between Europe and Africa. The relationships between races are not perfect in practice, but the unprejudiced visitor to Angola comes away with memories of one example after another of black and white men working together, building their own homes together, studying together, and recreating together. One of the great agricultural co-operatives in the south will eventually total 9,000 families—white, black, and coloured. Wherever you go, school children of all racial strains may be seen in classes with a coloured teacher. I saw black, white and coloured refugees being cared for together in Luanda by white Portuguese of the Red Cross, Caritas, and Catholic Action, most of whom flew from Portugal for the purpose. Refugees were being housed in modern flats, their children were being taught in special schools. The 100,000 odd refugees who fled to the Congo were fleeing not from the army but from the area of battle and from the terrorists who murdered white and black indiscriminately. The Red Cross reported from

Leopoldville that these refugees, far from showing signs of oppression and undernourishment, were mostly healthy and well cared for. Even Portugal's sternest critics have to admit that the refugees themselves testify that they were fleeing as much from the rebels as from anyone else. Most of them crossed the border because they were cut off from Luanda. But some 10,000 did get there—thus choosing the protection of the Portuguese.

## Labour Conditions

In an attempt to secure a clearer picture of the labour system, I talked to American, Dutch, Danish, Italian and Portuguese business men, priests, diplomats, officials, journalists and professional men—some of whom had lived in Angola for many years. Some were actual employers of 'contract labour'. The rest had watched it at work. As a result of these enquiries, I formed the following picture:

Forced labour, in the strict sense, ceased to exist long ago. The system of 'contracted labour' applies only to the shiftless who will not provide properly for themselves and their families. The test is whether or not they can pay a small annual tax, amounting to less than £3. In a sense, the native does not need to work and is often reluctant to do so. The trees around him will feed him and his family. Too often, the husband is prepared to idle and to enjoy the fruits of his wife's labours. If native Angolans are to take their place in a developing society, they must, say the Portuguese, be made to do their share of the work. The conditions imposed by Portuguese law on employers of 'contracted labour', as it is called, are rigorous. So much so that many employers are dropping this system of recruitment, as it is far too expensive for them.

The contracted labourer is usually paid the same as the voluntary worker. In addition, if he has to move away from home, for a maximum of six months in some cases and twelve months in others, the employer must provide transport for him and his family should they wish to accompany him. The employer must also provide a hospital, certain carefully prescribed amounts of living space, and separate rooms for married couples. I have seen this type of small hospital, and found it compared well with our smaller local hospitals in this country. Employers cannot recruit contract labour without a licence; such licences are now granted so rarely that the whole system is dying. Firms like the Diamond Mining Company find that already their voluntary labourers are more than double the number of contracted workers. The general verdict of the non-Portuguese businessmen to whom I spoke—including those who do not employ contracted labour—was that, on the whole, the Angolan natives' conditions are equivalent to those obtaining in most other African countries. This view was confirmed by American journalists and consular officials who have had experience of many parts of the continent.

Contracted labourers can earn about 35s. a week. This must be seen against the fact that it costs a man only 1s. 3d. a day to feed himself. Half his earnings are held for him until the end of his contract, and he takes it home as a lump sum. In the tribal system, the returning labourers' lump sums are often paid to the tribal chief who then purchases agricultural equipment, for example, for the whole community.

But while I record all this to redress the factual balance, it would, of course, be absurd to pretend that there has not been a disgraceful history of past abuses. There was undoubtedly a time when exploitation and vicious ill-treatment of native workers was very common. Nor has the abuse of the system been cleared up yet by any means. There has been plenty of illegal beating and bullying, more by the smaller employer than by the larger company. In the main, the quality of the Portuguese District Officer has been of a high order. It is in the lower grades of administrative framework that corruption has been admitted. The *chefe de posto* tends to be the more likely culprit. But there is little he can do without the aid of a corrupt tribal chief ready to sell his own people down the line. The Government has been concerned to clean up the hideous triangle of illegally operating employers, corrupt officials, and tribal chiefs out to line their pockets. Over the past decade the situation has improved substantially, and numbers of junior officials have been dismissed. It is admitted that natives have time and again been grossly cheated when selling their products in the concessionary markets—usually by liaison between the natives' own sales representatives, a crooked market official, and a crooked buyer. An Overseas Ministry executive put it to me thus: 'At least this much good has come out of the uprising—that we have been made to face up even more determinedly to the weaknesses of our system. This cheating, for instance, is something that will never happen again.'

Among the younger senior officials whom I met, I found men dedicated to the rapid development of the native communities, and who are determined to learn from the errors of the past. They recognise that too much emphasis has been placed on the political suitability of white Portuguese coming to work in Angola; that some selection according to a man's moral record is more to the point; that his politics will take care of themselves when he is up to his neck in hard work; that he should be a man capable of giving moral leadership to the natives. A step is being taken in this direction by the encouragement of the concept of the soldier-colonist. The well-disciplined soldier, retiring in the province where he has served, will tend, under this scheme, to settle down there. He will often be a man capable of a high degree of good example, and will be available too as a kind of territorial reservist in case of trouble.

One of the elements making for a genuine multi-racial situation in Angola is that the white settler often has an equal or even inferior material background to that of the native. A natural inter-racial relationship is more noticeable in the country than in the town, of course, and everywhere there are the usual barriers of class, social standing and education. These are, however, quite different from racial snobbery, which has little meaning in a Portuguese context.

Some 40 per cent of the administrative officials in Angola are non-white. In Guinea and Cap Verde the proportion is nearer 90 per cent. Some 500 Africans are studying at universities in Portugal. In the African territories you will meet non-whites of very high standing including, for instance, an Inspector of Political Affairs, a newspaper proprietor, a Chief of the Technical Section of the Public Works Department. In the plantations you will find a few Africans who can justly be termed rich. Everywhere you will meet non-white nurses, policemen, engineers, airport managers, chemists, doctors, wharf inspectors, farmers; the Negro farmer who has built his house and established his plantation with credit from local white merchants; the white father who leaves substantial property to half-caste sons. Under the assimilation system there were only 70,000 *assimilados* out of 4,000,000 Angolan natives. But many thousands more were ripe for it. They preferred the intermediary stage of 'improved' native because full assimilation would have entailed greater legal obligations, including higher taxation.

## Partnership

Throughout history, society has always been unkind to the half-caste. But he finds his dignity in Portuguese communities and through them may find his place in the future, for the Portuguese half-caste is a natural bridgehead between Europe and Africa. I have often supported the principle that the white man's role in Africa is to train native peoples to the point where they can take over the reins of government, and then to become the black man's servant, adviser, and technical expert. But in Portuguese Africa I believe it is natural and right to think, not in terms of white serving black, but of a genuine white and black partnership. In this, Portuguese

Africa is probably unique. Portugal's multi-racial traditions are not Salazarist formulas for the justification of a continuing colonisation. The very Portugal whose escutcheon is sullied by the history of the Angolan slave trade (and there are two sides even to that story) has to her credit the laying of the foundations for multi-racial Brazil. It is true that in Brazil Negroes were outnumbered by the whites, whereas in Angola the reverse is the case. But the number of Angolan Africans fighting against the Portuguese is a very small minority, and, if asked what they mean by 'independence', usually say something that means in effect 'unlimited cash in the bank, derived from plundering and expropriation of the whites' (see A. W. Sire's letter to the *Tablet*, of 22 July 1961).

I am satisfied that the overwhelming majority of Africans in Angola are not seething with desire to expel the Portuguese. They have innumerable grievances and complaints, like any other African community, many of them thoroughly well founded. But I do not believe that they want to throw the baby out with the bath water, or, to mix the metaphor, to kill the goose that lays such golden eggs as may be available. Portugal's material achievements in Angola are extraordinary when a fair-minded critic takes into account the extreme poverty of the mother country. The best of the co-operative settlements in Angola and Mozambique, yielding more efficient production and a sense of proprietorship for the inhabitants, are at Cela, Inhamisso, Loge, Bembe, Damba and Caconda. At Cela the Portuguese drained 125,000 acres of swamp, and now several hundred families live there in 12 villages with their own churches and schools. At Inhamissa, they dried out a huge malaria ridden swamp, and the co-operative now produces bumper crops of bananas, rice and wheat. A vast operation was carried out to dam the Limpopo River and thus establish a home for what will ultimately amount to 6,000 families.

It was Portuguese foresight that years ago brought the

three Angolan railway systems together, rebuilt them according to the same gauge, and extended them with a view to attracting foreign investments. This was at a time when the prospect of getting money from abroad was very remote. Today, in consequence, German and American firms are bringing 40,000,000 dollars into Coima to exploit the huge deposits of iron ore. Production has doubled in four years in Angola, and her building programme results in the estimate that the ratio of built-up areas per thousand inhabitants as between Angola and British East Africa is as follows: Angola 76; Kenya 51; Uganda 17; and Tanganyika 14. Great progress has been made in the field of public health; sleeping sickness, which has killed many of the best men over a period of centuries, is now virtually destroyed. The World Health Organisation has commended Portuguese Africa for outstanding success in treating leprosy. Proportionately, Angola treats twice as many of her lepers as Ghana, Tanganyika, and Kenya treat of theirs, and her success in this field is well in advance of Nigeria's.

## Defects and the Church

There could be plenty of ground for high hopes in Portuguese Africa generally, but only if certain fundamental defects are faced and cured. Broadly speaking, while the Catholic Church in most mission countries seeks to build on indigenous cultures, baptising and purifying them, and marrying them to Christian civilisation, Portugal still works on the basis that the best way to Christianise is to Europeanise. There is firm respect for native tradition: the *indigenato* system leaves the native free to live by his own tribal law if he so wishes. But it is for positive construction on the basis of the native tradition that the Bishop of Beira has pleaded. The bishops have played their part in multi-racial development in many ways. There is no doubt that their insistence on the sanctity of family life has done much to make improvements in the labour system, especially in preventing the splitting up of families. Out of 452 priests in Angola seventy are Africans, and only seven of them have associated themselves with rebel movements. There are also thirty-eight black brothers and eighty-eight nuns. These numbers are nevertheless woefully small, and the reason is Portugal's failure to educate more than a small proportion of the native population. Her own great poverty accounts for it in part. Moreover, the Angolan does not tend to be bright, and most of those who are educated 'stick' at the second year. But the younger members of the administration are concerned about the effect on native education of the Missionary Agreement of 1940 between Portugal and the Holy See. It insists so much on *Portuguese* missionaries and education that (a) the best elements in the African's own make-up are left undeveloped, and (b) the number of mission-aries, all of whom are naturally teachers, is inevitably restricted, for Portuguese vocations are still comparatively few. The situation is paradoxical in a multi-racial atmosphere, and comparatively easy to correct. A marriage between British and African cultures is a mixed marriage indeed. But a cultural marriage of Portuguese Catholicism and those innumerable elements in the African soul capable of baptism would seem to be the most natural thing in the world. Many Portuguese will say that this is precisely what happens already. On the higher social and intellectual levels, perhaps. But for the masses of the people, this cultural (as opposed to social) marriage has yet to be consummated.

## Democracy?

I do not believe that Dr. Salazar will ever want to give a democratic structure to Portugal and her oversea territories. He is a legendary, quasi-mystical figure whose people can love and be violently angry with him at one and the same time. He is a great 'headmaster' who cannot bring himself to realise that his boys have left the school whose books he has balanced so well. The Bishop of Oporto, now in exile as a result of his own less than tactful methods, undoubtedly knew the right answer. He envisaged the development of a Christian Democratic opposition, capable of effective and constructive criticism, as the best means of bringing the people into active and adult partnership with their government. He has much in common with the Bishop of Beira, and upon such men the Church in Portugal could build a great future. They command the respect, not only of the faithful, but also of the normally anti-clerical liberals.

There are far too many people in political detention and there is no doubt that the Security Police (the PIDE) are too much of a law unto themselves. Stories of torture and murder in the PIDE prisons are hard to prove or disprove. Frankly, I believe such things happen, as is almost inevitable in any secret police organisation. It is plainly imperative that the PIDE should be fundamentally reformed and integrated into the regular police (like Scotland Yard's Special Branch), or into the army (like our military intelligence units).

Many thinking Portuguese recognise that they are not built for outright democracy on the British pattern. Many who remember the hatred, terror, assassination and degradation of pre-Salazar Portugal are slow to want to see the end of the man who restored stability. But even his closest supporters are hungry for some sort of change now. The Portuguese, who are always at their best and most dogged when their backs are against the wall, can erupt with violent impatience when they feel conscious that they are being relegated too long to adolescent status. What will happen after Salazar? Another statesman once said: '*Après moi, le déluge.*' Somehow, before he dies, he must leave as his last will and testament the foundations for a governmental structure lying somewhere between benevolent dictatorship and outright democracy. Portugal, with her great Christian tradition, her sense of family, her power of understanding humanity in all its shapes and sizes, has a unique part to play in introducing a reunited Christian Europe to the emergent nations of Africa.

# POLITICS OF A REVOLT

## PATRICIA McGOWAN PINHEIRO

### Historical background

THE Portuguese boast they have been in Africa for 400 years. This however is an over-simplification; in Angola penetration and effective occupation of the whole territory are considerably less than a century old, and resistance to Portuguese occupation has never been thoroughly subdued. In the light of what has actually taken place over the last eighty years it is clear that the present conflict in Angola is due to no sudden invasion from outside but is the logical continuation of a struggle that has never been interrupted for very long. It was only in the 1870s that the actual military conquest of what is now Angola was launched. Till then Portuguese settlements were mainly on the coast and only in a few places inland, although the Portuguese claimed sovereignty over the entire area lying between the coast of Angola on the west and the coast of Mozambique on the east. 'In the interior the tribes remained in complete rebellion,' admits the officially approved Portuguese school history.[1]

With British penetration of the area now known as Rhodesia, an impetus was given to Portuguese settlement. Fearing that unsubjugated areas would encourage other European nations to claim further territory, the Portuguese began to step up the process of conquest. A series of

PATRICIA McGOWAN PINHEIRO was born in Lancashire in 1925 of an Irish mother and a Portuguese father. At the University of Liverpool she studied law which she continued after the war at McGill University, Montreal. Miss Pinheiro lived for several years in the United States and Canada and was a journalist in Czechoslovakia and Eastern Europe. For many years she has been interested in the politics of Portugal and her colonies and wrote, with Peter Fryer, *Oldest Ally: A Portrait of Salazar's Portugal;* she is now translating Aquilino Ribeiro's novel, banned by Salazar, *When the Wolves Howl* and working on a modern history of the Portuguese African colonies.

bloody operations commenced which lasted throughout the remaining years of the Monarchy and the first nine years of the Republic.

By 1919, the official historians declare, Portuguese domination of Angola was 'completely secured and the whole province was pacified'.[2] Three years later effective administrative occupation started. In other words Portuguese control over Angolan territory is only four years older than the present dictatorship in Portugal itself.

Before 1922, however, the military campaigns in Angola were in no sense an uninterrupted series of triumphs, and had it not been for agreement among the European Powers at the end of the First World War to prevent the export of arms to Africans, full-scale armed resistance might well have continued in Angola.

Every step met with bitter resistance which was only overcome with the utmost ferocity. African chiefs were killed, and the occupiers at once introduced an entirely new tribal structure showing scant respect for native custom or tradition. Currently the Portuguese authorities are anxious to present a different picture. But the true state of affairs has been publicly admitted by no less than one of Salazar's colonial ministers:

Defending the ideas realised in certain African colonies, there are many who wish to base the peaceful exercise of our sovereignty on the traditional authority of the black chiefs. But the truth is that the military and then the administrative occupation has destroyed in great part the original hierarchies and cadres.[3]

Despite effective occupation, however, there took place in Angola both in 1922 and in 1939 large-scale uprisings and in the years between many lesser skirmishes.

As for white Angolans, most of these have not been in Angola long. At the beginning of this century there were some 9,000 whites in Angola. By 1940 the number had reached 40,000 and by 1950 there were 79,000.[4] In the last ten years the number of whites is estimated to have risen to 200,000.

## The Growth of Political Protest

The first examples of African political resistance to the Portuguese took the form of journals produced and read by the tiny handful of educated Angolans in the towns. But these were soon closed down, printing presses seized and those responsible deported.

One of the earliest political organisations in which Angolans took part was the *Liga Africana*. To give the League encouragement the second session of the Third Pan-African Congress in 1923 was transferred to Lisbon and held under the auspices of the *Liga Africana*. The Congress report describes the *Liga Africana* as:

an actual federation of all the indigenous associations scattered throughout the five provinces of Portuguese Africa and representing several million individuals. . . . This *Liga Africana* which functions in Lisbon in the very heart of Portugal, so to speak, has a commission from all the other native organisations and knows how to express to the Government in no ambiguous terms but in a highly dignified manner all that should be said to avoid injustice or bring about the repeal of harsh laws. That is why the *Liga Africana* of Lisbon is the director of the Portuguese African movement, but not only in the good sense of the word, but without any appeal to violence and without leaving constitutional limits.[5]

In 1923 Portugal was still a democratic republic. Three years later in 1926 the present regime was established. Conditions in the colonies had been bad enough already—now Salazarism was to build and entrench Portuguese colonialism on the foundations laid down by the previous regimes, both monarchist and republican. The Angolans were not slow to react.

In 1929 in Luanda the *Liga Nacional Africana* (L.N.A.) was founded by a number of illegal and semi-legal organisations which had existed in the colony for many years. In the same year the *Grémio Africano* was founded. This was later called the *Associação Regional dos Naturais de Angola* (ANANGOLA). For the next ten years African protest found expression through these organisations. By the 1940s, however, differences of opinion began to be felt in the L.N.A. Hitherto that organisation had confined itself to demands for reform; now there was talk about the need for new methods of righting grievances which required the direct participation of the urban masses. There were demands inside the L.N.A. for its transformation into a mass organisation in which 'natives' would take part as well as 'assimilados'.

The authorities responded to these signs of unrest according to the usual pattern: threats, pressure of all kinds and introduction of police agents. Finally the elected leaders were replaced by administrative committees nominated by the colony's Governor-General.

Another attempt at legal organisation by Angolans was the *Associação Africana do Sul de Angola* (AASA) founded by railway workers in Nova Lisboa. However, its militant programme was soon interfered with by the authorities and the organisation was rendered ineffective.

After the Second World War political awareness among Angolan Africans began to spread further. Although forced labour, economic exploitation and deprivation of civil rights had generally worsened in the colonies since the advent to power of Salazar, and it was not until the 1950s that there began to be imposed in the colonies the same strict censorship and secret police activity that was characteristic of Portugal. In Angola immediately after the war there was thus considerably more freedom of thought and discussion than in Portugal—though the benefits of such a state of affairs were felt only by the white population and the tiny minority of *assimilados*. The general defeat of Fascism in Europe, despite Salazar's survival, had its repercussions in this distant corner of Africa. Foreign books, especially from Brazil, dealing with the origins of Fascism and the fight for national liberation began to come into the country. News had also started to trickle into Angola of the growing independence movements in the African colonies of other European Powers.

In consequence the younger generation of Angolans became impatient with the reformist ideas of their elders.

They began to talk about the need for ending the barrier between 'native' and *'assimilado'* and urged the need to form African mass organisations to work for Angolan independence.

The *Partido da Luta Unida dos Africanos de Angola* (PLUA) was the first revolutionary political party which planned to operate as an illegal mass organisation. A manifesto was issued calling on Africans to join underground groups and unite in a broad movement for the liberation of the colony. In December 1956 leaders of PLUA and other organisations met together in Luanda to form the *Movimento Popular de Libertação de Angola* (M.P.L.A.). The new movement was to be a mass political organisation working inside Angola and its founders were Africans who had never left their country.

Meanwhile in 1954, outside Angola, there had been formed the *União das Populações do Norte de Angola*, which in 1958 was renamed the *União das Populações de Angola* (UPA). This organisation was founded in Leopoldville in the then Belgian Congo and reflected the aspirations of Angolan nationalists among the half million or so Angolan migrant workers who had gone to the Congo in search of jobs. Because of the important military role of UPA in the present conflict in Angola, both the Salazar Government and certain foreign observers have attempted to present Angolan nationalism as an alien importation from outside the colony sponsored by foreign, probably Communist, sources.

But the activity of the M.P.L.A. since its foundation demonstrates the indigenous character of the nationalist movement. Among the M.P.L.A.'s first activities was the creation of underground schools to teach illiterates how to read and write. By means of these contacts it engaged in continual agitation and propaganda and leaflets were issued putting forward its policy. The M.P.L.A.'s prestige grew and began to be reflected inside the legal L.N.A. and ANANGOLA where dissatisfaction was coming to a head.

A further nationalist organisation was founded in 1958: the *Movimento para a Independência Nacional de Angola* (MINA). This later fused with the M.P.L.A.

Two other important organisations of the Angola people are illegal trade unions: the *União dos Trabalhadores e Operários Negros de Angola* (UTONA) which has its underground headquarters inside the colony; and the *União dos Trabalhadores Angolanos* (UNTA) formed in 1954, which has its headquarters in Leopoldville and is affiliated to the Conference of Nationalist Organisations of the Portuguese Colonies.

Another nationalist party which has its headquarters in Leopoldville is the ALIAZO, the Zombo People's Alliance, an organisation of the Zombo people in northern Angola who have emigrated to the Congo. ALIAZO claims the support of some two-thirds of the million Angolans living between Uige and the Congo frontier. It is led by André Massaki, a Protestant journalist, who is its chairman. Together with vice-chairman Antoine Matumona, Massaki recently visited Europe in an attempt to persuade Western Governments to change their policy towards Salazar.

*Armed struggle becomes inevitable*

On 29 March 1959 the Portuguese authorities struck and several hundred people, including leaders of the M.P.L.A., were arrested. It was at this time that to avoid arrest and the complete decapitation of their organisation that many of the M.P.L.A. leaders were compelled to leave the country and carry on their work from places of exile. Three trials followed in which a total of fifty-seven persons were accused of 'attempts against the external security of the State and the unity of the nation'.

Shortly afterwards the Portuguese began to increase military reinforcements in Angola. For the first time Angolan political resistance was officially recognised and in May Salazar himself called on the other colonial powers to join in concerted action against what he called 'flames lit from abroad'. But neither of the two main nationalist organisations concealed the fact that, like all other African movements, they intended to seek the active sympathy and support of the continent-wide anti-colonial movement. Leaders of both the M.P.L.A. and UPA began to attend international African conferences and seek their support.

In May 1960 a conference was held in Africa between exiled leaders of the M.P.L.A. and delegates from the organisations within Angola. Those working inside the colony were eager to start immediate action against the Portuguese. The exiles however felt that before this path was taken every measure should be explored to arrive at a peaceful solution and meanwhile the unity of all nationalist organisations should be sought. An appeal was launched for the creation of an Angolan Liberation Front.

On 13 June the M.P.L.A. addressed a declaration to the Portuguese Government requesting a peaceful solution of the colonial question. The Portuguese answered with intensified military preparations and mass arrests in Luanda, Lobito, Malange and Dalatando. Troop reinforcements and air force units were posted to the frontier regions. By July the situation had grown tenser than ever and Portuguese troops began terror raids on the African quarters of Luanda, where they attacked inhabitants, set fire to houses and tortured women and children. On 13 September 1960 the M.P.L.A. issued an appeal to the member States of the United Nations to discuss the Angolan situation and to put pressure on Portugal. In November twenty-eight nationalists from Cabinda were shot in the courtyard of a Luanda prison. The M.P.L.A. issued a second appeal to the Angolan population for the unity of all patriotic parties, organisations and personalities. On 6 December 1960, the M.P.L.A., together with nationalist organisations from other Portuguese colonies, held a Press conference in London. The M.P.L.A. leaders warned that the Portuguese Government had ignored all efforts at negotiations and was actively preparing for war against the Angolan people. This attitude, they pointed out, left only one alternative open to the Angolans—direct action against Portuguese colonialism.

On 4 February direct action started. Sixty-odd foreign journalists were in Luanda anxiously awaiting the arrival of the *Santa Maria* with Captain Galvão in command. M.P.L.A. supporters seized the opportunity and attacked the prisons, the broadcasting station and a military barracks. Battle raged for three days. On 5 February alone more than 3,000 Africans were killed. From that moment onward pitched battles began to take place in various parts of Angola, until in March armed uprising began in the Congo region of northern Angola.

*Angolan Nationalists and other Portuguese colonies*

From its early days leaders of the M.P.L.A. had kept in close touch with the nationalist movement of Portuguese Guinea, the *Partido Africano de Independência* (PAI). Both these organisations agreed on the need to make their movements known abroad and they helped to form the *Movimento Anticolonialista* (MAC) composed of Africans from the Portuguese colonies who were living abroad. Its aims were: to study the needs of the nationalist organisations; to work for unity of action among the liberation movements of the Portuguese colonies; and to train themselves as reserves for the struggle being carried on inside their countries. MAC took part in the Second Conference of African Peoples and made world opinion aware for the first time of what was going on in the Portuguese colonies. Eventually MAC was dissolved to be replaced by the *Frente Revolucionária Africana para a Independência Nacional* (FRAIN) open to all organisations of the Portuguese colonies which were actively engaged in struggle against colonialism.

In December 1960 representatives from Angola, Guinea and Goa, meeting in London, announced their decision to call a conference of nationalist organisations from all the eight Portuguese colonies in order to set up a permanent co-ordinating committee.

This conference took place from 18–20 April 1961 at Casablanca and founded the Conference of Nationalist Organisations of the Portuguese Colonies (CONCP). FRAIN was thereupon dissolved. There were fourteen delegates present from ten organisations representing all the Portuguese colonies except Macau and Timor. The M.P.L.A. chairman Mário de Andrade was elected chairman. A permanent secretariat was constituted with Marcelino dos Santos of Mozambique as its General Secretary. The conference appealed to leaders of African and Asian States to bring their influence to bear to end the war in Angola. It decided that the principles upon which CONCP activities would be based were those laid down at the various Afro-Asian Conferences that followed Bandung in 1955. It further decided: to struggle for the complete ending of Portuguese colonialism and all forms of oppression; to work for solidarity and unity between all nationalist organisations in the Portuguese colonies; to work for a common front in each colony; and to secure international support for the struggle for national independence.

Meeting in New Delhi in October last the CONCP reported on its achievements over the previous six months. Substantial material, diplomatic and moral help had been received in response to the Casablanca appeal. Examples were:

Ghana had banned Portuguese ships and aircraft from her harbours and airfields; Indonesia had recalled her ambassador from Lisbon; Senegal had broken off diplomatic relations with Portugal; Dahomey had liberated the Portuguese fort of São João Baptista de Ajudá. Concerning Angola, the New Delhi statement added that efforts were being made to create a united front between the UPA and the M.P.L.A. and that a voluntary corps to help Angolan refugees had been created to take charge of the thousands of refugees in the Congo, known as CVAAR.

The CONCP concluded its statement by appealing to every country for material help for the Angolan fighters;

medical supplies and food; direct pressure on the Portuguese Government; the banning of arms supplies to Portugal; United Nations' sanctions against Portugal.[6]

## The M.P.L.A. moves to Leopoldville

After M.P.L.A. leaders had been arrested or forced to flee into exile in 1959 the movement's headquarters were situated in Conakry in the Republic of Guinea. Its distance from the scene of operations in northern Angola and lack of co-ordination with the UPA have given rise to a number of misconceptions about the M.P.L.A.'s role in the present struggle. Since 30 October 1961 however, the M.P.L.A.'s headquarters has been officially transferred to Leopoldville where Mário de Andrade has explained recently the reasons for the transfer and outlined the M.P.L.A.'s activities and prospects. He declared that the central point of all M.P.L.A. policy was its constant effort to seek unity of action between all Angolan nationalist forces and that the executive committee of the M.P.L.A. was ready to make all necessary concessions so that there could be immediately constituted an Angolan Liberation Front. He called on the leaders of all Angolan nationalist movements to come together and draw up a political platform which would help to speed up the struggle for liberation.

As far as foreign policy was concerned Andrade made it clear that this was based on 'positive neutralism' and aimed at winning the sympathy and support of all sectors of the world for the Angolan independence struggle, though it was natural that the M.P.L.A. should look first to African solidarity.

Regarding the present armed struggle Andrade declared that the Angolan people were the principal motive force. He outlined the actual course of events and stated that the M.P.L.A.-led actions of February 1961 had been the spark which had encouraged the northern peoples to rise in the following month. M.P.L.A. guerrillas were active in the districts of Cuanza-Norte, Luanda, Congo and

Malange. Their aim from the outset had been the paralysis of the colonial economy, the liquidation of the administrative apparatus and military resistance to the enemy. These objectives had been attained in practically all the regions where M.P.L.A. militia were operating. Wherever Portuguese armed force, equipped with all the best modern weapons, was too strong the guerrillas had evacuated the occupied areas, taking with them the entire civilian population into the bush. The M.P.L.A.'s military organisation. It was headed by a Revolutionary Committee responsible for all aspects of the armed struggle and was at present in the course of establishing itself on Angolan territory.

The population was co-operating with the M.P.L.A. militia and was engaging in the sabotage of bridges and roads, the liquidation of enemy agents, the transport of food and ammunition for combat units, reconnaissance activities, the destruction of settlers' plantations and the safeguard of health.

The CVAAR, sponsored by CONCP, but set up initially by the M.P.L.A., was helping the 160,000 refugees in the Congo. CVAAR had undertaken a considerable task: disease prevention and hygiene; free distribution of medical supplies, clothes and food; the fight against illiteracy.

The weaknesses in organisation of the Angolan struggle, Andrade concluded, could only be overcome by the united action of all political organisations. This unity was already growing especially among young people whatever their political allegiance might be.

## UPA and the Struggle in the North

Although M.P.L.A. leaders have met and held talks with the leaders of UPA, so far the latter has not committed itself to united action with them, nor is it affiliated to CONCP. The differences between the two principal Angolan nationalist organisations arise from their differing compositions and the circumstances in which each has developed. The people of the northern region of Angola have always been closely associated with the population across the border in the former Belgian Congo. Historically they were part of one nation and the frontier dividing them is one more example of the unnaturalness of the borders established in Africa by European colonialism. It was to be expected therefore that once people on the Angolan side of the frontier realised they could earn better wages and avoid the rigours of Portuguese rule by crossing the frontier, emigration should take place. In the Congo they learned that Africans could become independent of Europeans.

Most of the migrants were peasants and had no experience of political struggle inside Angola itself. An additional factor influencing these northern Angolans was the existence of a large number of Baptist and other Protestant missions on both sides of the frontier. Many Africans received a certain amount of education in these missions and learned to compare the attitudes of the largely British and American Protestant clergy with those of the Portuguese and Italian Catholic missionaries who in the main supported the Portuguese regime.

UPA is largely a peasant party and its strength is confined to the northern area of Angola, its ties with the people of these areas being tribal rather than political. Its chairman, Roberto Alvaro Holden, was born in San Salvador in northern Angola.

Roberto Holden, the leader of UPA, went to the Congo as a boy and received his secondary education there. He worked in the Finance Department of the Belgian administration in Leopoldville, Stanleyville and Bukava. Several visits to Angola persuaded him that something should be done to liberate his people from Portuguese rule and in 1954 he and six companions founded the UPA. The organisation claims 40,000 registered members and its paper *La Nation Angolaise* appears fortnightly in four languages: Portuguese, French and two African tongues. UPA headquarters are in Leopoldville and a New York office is being set up with the help of the Republic of Tunisia.

The UPA programme published in 1960 condemns racial

oppression and discrimination in Angola, the slave economy
and cultural obscurantism.   It protests against the despatch
of Portuguese troops to Angola, the use of napalm by the
Portuguese Air Force, the man hunts organised against
Angolan nationalists, and the summary deportations and
executions:

Between Angolans and Portuguese [the programme says]
there exist none of the fundamental characteristics which
would permit them to be identified as a single people. . . .
What does exist are antagonisms aggravated day by day by
racial discrimination, the inequality of the most elementary
rights, cynical exploitation and oppression without precedent
in colonial history. . . .   What does exist is the growing and
unceasing revolt of the Angolans.[7]

The ferocity of Angolan resistance to the Portuguese has
been interpreted as evidence that Angola nationalism, and
particularly UPA, is bitterly anti-white.   However, it seems
clear that Holden and his followers make a distinction
between Portuguese whites and American or British whites.
An American journalist who spent some time with the
UPA guerrillas and went into UPA-occupied territory
reports:

I, as a white, was warmly welcomed.   This was true in the
villages as well as later among rebel troops.   Holden Roberto
and his colleagues had told me in numerous interviews that
they were not leading an anti-European movement.   The
revolution is not anti-white; it is simply—and brutally—
anti-Portuguese.[8]

The same writer describes a UPA leaflet which he saw
distributed among villagers in the interior of Angola.   It
was a sheet of general instructions written in the Kikongo
language and contained ten points.   Among them were
the following:

Each village should select an individual to be responsible
for the transmission of information and receipt of UPA
commands.   Such a person was to express opinions 'not
according to his own views, but the views of the whole
population'.   There was to be no stealing by UPA soldiers.

No item seized from the Portuguese should be kept. There should be co-operation and mutual respect between old and young. All the money the people could lay their hands on should be sent to UPA in Leopoldville, 'because if we do not have money our work for independence cannot continue'.[9]

## Leaders of the M.P.L.A. and their Programme

The Portuguese authorities were the first to call the M.P.L.A. Communists and to allege they received financial aid from the Soviet bloc. But this sort of accusation is used indiscriminately by the Salazarists against all their opponents; more serious is the fact that this allegation has been taken up and circulated by some foreign observers. The attitudes and aims of the M.P.L.A. leaders are no secret. They have been stated publicly on many occasions, in both the organisation's long-term programme and in speeches and writings by its leaders. Of course, many of the M.P.L.A. leaders are in jail, notably its honorary chairman Dr. Agostinho Neto, Angola's leading poet whose works have appeared in many languages.

Best-known abroad of the M.P.L.A.'s leaders who are not in jail is Mário Pinto de Andrade, the organisation's chairman.

Less well-known in Britain and America is the name of the M.P.L.A.'s general secretary, Viriato Francisco Clemente Cruz, who is thirty-three years old and particularly interesting because he learned his politics entirely inside Angola which he did not leave for any length of time until he was forced to flee from arrest in 1959. Viriato Cruz was responsible for founding the journal *A Mensagem* which was banned after its second issue and Cruz was dismissed from his Government post. He was one of the founders of the M.P.L.A. and since he fled abroad has travelled widely in Europe, Africa and Asia and has visited China and the Soviet Union.

This latter fact has often been seized on to indicate the M.P.L.A.'s political affiliations. But in an important address to the Rome Congress of Negro Writers in 1958, he outlined his political ideas at some length.

The unity of the Africans is the most powerful arm on our continent, of the struggle against colonialism. Their unity with each other will be an indispensable condition for material and spiritual progress as well as for securing freedom and the peaceful work of our peoples. This is a statement which, because it is simple and often repeated, already seems a platitude, but from which only we, the Africans, know how to deduce immense practical value, because we have present in our memory all our experience and the bitterness which is an instinct with us.[10]

Cruz went on to discuss the immense importance for Africans of the economic achievements of the Soviet bloc where 'coloured peoples under a socialist regime' had helped to prove that Cecil Rhodes's 1800 years were not needed in order to catch up with Europe.[11]

These ideas put forward by Viriato Cruz are also to be found in the M.P.L.A.'s long-term programme. This gives special prominence to the question of unity with the rest of Africa and supports eventual union of African States. It stands for neutralism in the cold war, economic planning and nationalisation of much of the land.

The M.P.L.A., by far the most powerful in numerical strength, organisation, historical links and ideas, is therefore clearly not a movement to which can be attached any of the traditional cold war labels. It is rather an integral part of the most developed trend in the African awakening: an African nationalist movement influenced by what is most positive in both East and West, namely the economic achievements in undeveloped regions which have been exemplified in the Soviet Union and China, and the democratic political ideals of the West.

## NOTES

[1] António G. Matoso, *Compêndio de História de Portugal,* Lisbon, 1944, p. 416.
[2] Ibid., p. 417.
[3] Professor Armindo Monteiro, 'Grandes ideias directrizes da

governação ultramarina no período que decorreu entre as duas guerras mundiais (1919–1939)', *História da expansão portuguesa no mundo*, Lisbon, Agência Geral das Colónias, 1942, p. 445.

[4] *Anuário Estatístico do Ultramar,* 1958, Lisbon: Instituto Nacional de Estatistica, 1959.

[5] Quoted in George Padmore, *Pan-Africanism or Communism?* London, 1956, p. 141.

[6] *Statement by CONCP,* New Delhi, 25 October 1961.

[7] 'Les Mouvements Nationalistes Angolais', *Tam Tam*, Paris, no. 3–4, p. 104, 1961.

[8] Richard Mathews, 'A Visit to the Rebels of Angola', *The Reporter,* 28 September 1961.

[9] *Ibid.*

[10] Viriato Cruz, 'Des responsabilités de l'intellectuel noir', *Présence Africaine,* nos. 27–28, Tome II, p. 330.

[11] Ibid., p. 331.

# ANGOLAN DISUNITY*

## ANTOINE MATUMONA

FOR about the last ten months we have been witnessing, perhaps hopefully, the heroic armed struggle of our Angolan brothers in their own land. Today in this relative lull which may be the prelude to an intensification of the struggle—the future is unpredictable—let us see whether the Angolan people have in fact achieved, or are in the process of achieving their objective; if not, let us look for the real cause of failure.

Angolan nationalists' armed resistance to the atrocities of Portuguese soldiers, mostly in the north of Angola, was started by a liberation movement that is well-known in the Congolese capital: *L'União des Populacoes d'Angola*—UPA.

Not much is known about the origins of this movement but it seems that the UPA grew out of disagreement within the Sao Salvador tribe. At that time, around 1954, they wanted to choose a king (Ntotela). The Catholic members of the tribe insisted that the future King should be of the Catholic faith in accordance with tradition. The Protestants, on the other hand, wanted him to be a Protestant like themselves. Here were two rival camps opposed to each other and there was no question of compromise. It was not long before the first group formed itself into a mutual aid association which became a political party in 1960: *Ngwizako-Ngwizani a kongo*. Its headquarters is at Leopoldville.

As for the Protestants, the second group, their first thought was for the need to consolidate. So they set about organising themselves and decided, in the process, that the

ANTOINE MATUMONA is Vice-Chairman of the Zombo People's Alliance (ALIAZO). He works for the *Courrier d'Afrique*, Leopoldville, from which paper this article has been taken and adapted, with the author's permission.

*Translated by S. M. Armstrong.

future king of the Sao Salvador ought not to be ignorant like his predecessors, but learned, liberal-minded and imbued with democratic principles. To attain this end it was obvious that travel and a foreign education would be necessary so Roberto Holden, now President of the UPA, was chosen for this purpose. After an energetic money raising campaign directed by Edouard Pinock, financial support was offered by Holden's family and by the Bazombo people and Holden went off abroad. He went first to Ghana; there his contacts with the leader of Pan-Africanism radically changed his whole outlook. From 'Ntolaism' he devolved rapidly to more liberal and republican ideas. He went post haste back to Brazzaville, summoned his 'chiefs' and without beating about the bush told them that monarchism was out of date and that in order to go along with contemporary trends they must now face up to the heavy task of winning back the independence of Angola.

On completion of this mission Holden hurried back to Ghana where he remained until the Congo became independent. The 'chiefs' returned to Leopoldville, founded the UPA which became the *União des Populacoes d'Angola* in 1958 and did not expand until Holden returned from Ghana. UPA then rapidly organised itself in Leopoldville —thanks to Holden's close friendship with Patrice Lumumba.

In the meantime, the Bazombo people, a large tribe of merchants and farmers who live in the northern province of Congo-Angola (or Portuguese Congo), had grouped themselves together with the Sao Salvador tribe, into one mutual help association known as *Assomizo,* of which Andre Massaki was the leading light. This mutual aid association turned into the Aliazo, the Zombo People's Alliance when the Congo became independent. Leopoldville is the headquarters of this party, of UPA and of the *Ngwizalo*.

Up to the beginning of 1961 these were the three main Angolan political organisations with headquarters in the

Congolese capital. But the picture would not be complete if we did not mention a further large political organisation, the M.P.L.A., the *Movimento Popular de Libertacão de Angola*. This group, whose leaders are Mário de Andrade and Viriato Cruz, chose Conakry for their headquarters. There was, nevertheless, a branch in Leopoldville and two months ago the M.P.L.A. leaders transferred their entire headquarters to Leopoldville. There will be more to say about this movement later on.

In less than a year two other political groups have established themselves in Leopoldville: *Le Mouvement de Defense des Interets Angolais* (M.D.I.A.) and the *N.T.O.-Abako*. This latter group had been set up by a few Abako tribe leaders who had territorial ambitions in northern Angola. The name of the party as well as the ethnic origin of its leaders confirms this statement. The leader is called Angelhinio Roberto.

The M.D.I.A. went through two main phases. It is in fact really the dissident group of UPA—the Mtala wing (after the name of its leader) in opposition to the Holden wing. It was founded by a group of young men, mostly from the Bazombo tribe, who constituted about three-quarters of the Executive Committee of UPA and broke away from it because they disapproved of Holden's isolationism and of his seizure of the Party. But his worst fault in their eyes was his nepotism—his brothers, cousins and uncles all held key posts in the party. They issued a *communiqué* to the Press publicly repudiating Holden. Holden, as a good leader, accepted this blow and was not cast down by such a sweeping exodus. As soon as these young men had left the UPA they went to offer their services to ALIAZO but after discussions on their integration into the Central Committee of ALIAZO had broken down, they decided to form their own group and founded the M.D.I.A.

The M.L.E.C. (*Mouvement pour la Libération de l'Enclave de Cabinda*) completes the list of Angolan political organisations.

So now Angola has seven political groups that share the same objective—the independence of Angola—but they are all working for it in different ways. Their few forces are dissipated and wasted and the chances of achieving their objective are thus reduced.

Each of the seven recognised Angolan parties working for the common objective, the economy of their national patrimony, has a separate plan of campaign. The M.D.I.A. believes that close co-operation with the Portuguese Government is the best way of regaining the independence of Angola, and they are prepared to pass through a 'community' stage. Jean Mtala, its leader,—in spite of the appalling atrocities suffered by the Angolan people at the hands of the Portuguese, both civil and military—firmly believes in 'frank and friendly' co-operation with the Fascist Salazar; he obtains financial and moral support from him, and he and his followers are educated in Lisbon at Portuguese Government expense. According to the M.D.I.A. the travel expenses for this and for a 'political tour' in September had been met by the Angolan people; but the Portuguese Vice-Consul in Leopoldville, Raoul da Souza, has supplied us with indisputable evidence to the contrary. An Angolan leader presented himself at the Portuguese embassy in Leopoldville, in August, to obtain his 'Portuguese passport'. The Vice-Consul took advantage of this opportunity and suggested that his party could easily 'negotiate with Salazar' through the intermediary of the Portuguese embassy in Leopoldville. The embassy would meet all travelling expenses. And he added: 'You must have heard about Jean-Pierre Mtala's trip to Lisbon—well, the Lisbon Government financed him'. This little piece of information is most revealing. It also shows the extent to which the Portuguese embassy in Leopoldville takes delight in disrupting Angola's political organisations by subtle and secret machinations.

The NTO-ABAKO and the NGWIZAKO use the same tactics as the M.D.I.A. Angelhinio Roberto, NTO-ABAKO leader, has just returned with forty scholarships from a trip to Lisbon. NGWIZAKO, too, has just had the 'privilege' of meeting Salazar and will doubtless return with scholarships for young Angolans.

The M.D.I.A., NTO-ABAKO and NGWIZAKO thus form a group of three who mean to 'co-operate closely' with the Portuguese authorities. According to a recent statement by the Portuguese Minister for Overseas Territories they are the only 'valid' representatives of the Angolan people.

The M.P.L.A., ALIAZO and the M.L.E.C. have also grouped themselves into a moderate and thoughtful trio. Before resorting to armed resistance against the Portuguese oppressors (a resistance against the brutality of the Portuguese Legion that could honestly be called 'defensive'), they attempted to resist by cultural means. The President of Portugal, Dr. Salazar, and the United Nations were pestered with a voluminous correspondence which demonstrated the falsity of the Portuguese claims that Angola is a Province of Portugal. At the same time they sent letters to Lisbon appealing to the Government to re-consider its claim to be realistic about the Angolan problems and to start negotiations before the masses became exasperated and rebelled. Unfortunately Salazar has always refused to consider the legitimate aspirations expressed in these innumerable petitions, or to consent to negotiate with the representatives of these parties. The United Nations resolutions are never acted upon and Portugal has been able to strengthen her position against the Angolans. If any reader would like to see the documents mentioned above, they are obtainable from the central offices of these parties.

It is true that the ALIAZO, M.L.E.C. and M.P.L.A. are moderate parties but they are also prepared for a defensive struggle with the Portuguese. They are still hoping to start genuine negotiations with Portugal but in a neutral country and under the auspices of the United Nations. The ALIAZO leader, Andre Massaki, does not think that the

Angolans and Portuguese will be able to solve their problem effectively without international arbitration.

On the other hand there is no longer any question of negotiation for UPA. It has decided to kick the Portuguese out of Angola without the help of any other Angolan political movement. This is not a surprise to those who have followed closely the statements of the UPA President. Holden's statements show that he wants to stand out amidst all the Angolan leaders, to give the impression that it is his party alone that is fighting at the front and that he alone is leader of the rebellion. But we must analyse the facts.

In early June, 1960, the Congo (Leopoldville) was preparing for its independence. Roberto Holden arrived in the Congolese capital from Ghana. He was received in triumph by the Angolans in Leopoldville who looked upon him as the Messiah come to assemble all his people and to set them up against the oppressor. At a banquet organised by the Bazombo people in honour of Roberto Holden, Andre Massaki, President of the ALIAZO, made a speech upon this theme. Holden replied that he would contact the influential Angolan personalities and explain to them his plan of campaign so that one single Angolan political party could be formed. A few days later, to everyone's great surprise, he broadcast over the Congolese radio and it was announced that he was leader of UPA. Holden was summoned by irritated Angolan notables who demanded an explanation. He replied forcefully: 'My party is like a church. I toll a bell; whoever wishes to may enter.'

The political organisations themselves blame all this confusion on to Roberto Holden. But the truth is that Holden is only responsible for three-quarters of this state of affairs and the other parties must share the responsibility for the remaining quarter.

One interesting fact emerges from the confusion: the Angolan political movements have always expressed the wish to unite in a Common Angolan Front. They have not only talked about this but have made considerable efforts to put it into practice.

On 1 November 1960 all the Angolan political organisations met in the hopes of realising their ideal, namely the regrouping of the political parties into one coherent whole. The UPA leaders took part in this meeting without Holden; the ALIAZO leaders and M.P.L.A. representatives were there. The M.L.E.C. sent a delegate and only the NGWIZAKO did not attend. As a result of this meeting, it was agreed that a common front was the only means of providing themselves with spokesmen who were qualified to speak for all Angola.

The Angolans were delighted and celebrated their first victory on the spot. A drafting committee was set up, composed of M.P.L.A., UPA and ALIAZO members. A telegram was sent to the President of the United Nations General Assembly protesting against the demonstrations that took place in Luanda on 4 November 1960 and a letter, signed by the three organisations, followed a few days later.

As soon as the Common Front had been formed the ALIAZO issued an illuminating *communiqué*. It said that although the ALIAZO was a racial party, formed by the union of the Zombo people for the safeguarding of their own interests, yet they were conscious of a larger nationalism. Therefore they were delighted by the realisation of a desire, shared with the other parties, to co-operate in a national *entente,* mutually respecting the opinions of each party—avoiding in this way futile discussions that could only detract from their common aim: the recovery of the independence and human dignity of the Angolan people. However, to avoid any confusion later on, the Central Committee of ALIAZO wished particularly to point out to its members and sympathisers that the formation of a Common Front of Angolan political parties did not mean that ALIAZO, or any other party, would be dissolved or change its policy. It warns them against the manoeuvres of any party that might try to profit from such an *entente* to confuse public opinion by spreading abroad false rumours in order to win converts, or even worse, to try and influence members of other parties. Such tactics would be contrary to the spirit of the 'agreement in principle' and harmful to the *entente*. ALIAZO still exists and will go on existing so that it can take its modest part in united action against the oppression of the Angolan people. It hopes that the other parties will give proof of the honesty of their intentions to work peacefully together to hasten the day they are all longing for—the day when Angola takes her place among the free nations.

This *communiqué* revealed the ALIAZO conception of the Common Front, a conception shared by UPA and the M.P.L.A.; they agreed to unite within the Front, but each would retain its own personality. Thus, they remain completely independent in internal affairs but in external affairs are represented by one organisation.

One month later, UPA left the Front. Roberto Holden had been in New York when it was formed and on his return he disapproved of the conduct of his closest collaborators. He accused them of involving UPA in too risky an adventure and as his word was law within the party, it was withdrawn from the Common Front. This was in December 1960.

The Common Front vegetated. Nevertheless, the joint efforts of the M.P.L.A. representatives—Jabes, George Freitas and A. Guiard amongst them—and of the ALIAZO leaders kept it going for a few months longer. During these months they worked furiously to supply the different African delegations at the United Nations with important documentation on Angola.

M. Emmanuel Dadet, Congo (Brazzaville) Ambassador to the United Nations chose to use this source of information for his able defence of the Angolan question before the United Nations. A misunderstanding finally resulted in the break up of the Front, and it was dissolved in February 1961. It was the only Common Front set up by the Angolans and even today, their leaders are unable to agree on any kind of joint Front. A few attempts have been made but all were doomed to failure.

It is thus that on 5 August 1960 the Central Committee

of NGWIZAKO met that of ALIAZO. At this meeting, NGWIZAKO wanted to set in motion attempts on both sides to fuse the two associations. NGWIZAKO also demonstrated its wish to collaborate closely with any party 'with the same ideology'. ALIAZO, on its side, proved more reticent because the end followed by NGWIZAKO has always been the revival of the former kingdom of Kongo, the only means—according to the leaders of NGWIZAKO—by which Angola could, peacefully, achieve independence. On 10 August, the spokesmen of both parties had to admit deadlock.

From May to July 1961, eight attempts at regrouping all the Angolan political organisations were registered, but all were fruitless. The last attempt took place on 12 July 1961 at the permanent office of ALIAZO. The M.L.E.C., the M.P.L.A. and ALIAZO were present at the meeting. The M.P.L.A. took the initiative by presenting a project; to this day the project is still in the study-stage.

While there is delay in coming to an agreement, the Portuguese soldiery sack, pillage and set fire to the bush, forests and villages, and kill and torture thousands of Angolan patriots, and the Angolan people, who are fighting at the front, are waiting for the recovery of their national patrimony.

The departure of young Angolan scholarship-holders, organised by the M.D.I.A. in co-operation with Lisbon, has already perplexed Angolans in Leopoldville. Up to the start of the popular rising in Angola 250 young Angolans are scattered among different Portuguese universities. All of 'Portuguese nationality' had left Angola for Portugal. What has happened to them today? Where are they? All 250 had been found 'suspect'. Accused of being 'activists', hunted like wild animals, persecuted by the PIDE, the famous secret police, they bolted and took refuge in other countries in Europe.

The departure of these students has astonished right-thinking Angolan circles, because all Angolans settled outside Angola are considered foreigners in the eyes of the

Lisbon Government. From this it follows that these scholarship-holders are foreigners and cannot travel legally on a Portuguese passport. In practice, they have been found to be holding Portuguese passports which have been refused to other Angolans who are in the same position as they are. Only recently, Andre Massaki, President-General of ALIAZO, was refused a Portuguese passport by the Vice-Consul Raoul de Souza. Domingos Vetokele, an 'assimilado' was also, to his great astonishment, refused the renewal of his Portuguese passport.

Angolan circles in the capital who keenly hope to re-instate their country, are worried by this policy of close 'co-operation' with Portugal—this 'independence in reverse' as an irate Angolan asserted. They are even more worried that the Portuguese activists in Leopoldville are thoroughly corrupting the Angolan leaders who are to be found at any time at the Portuguese Embassy in Leopoldville. And while Angolans are falling under Portuguese fire, their political leaders are prevaricating. Yet they know very well that there will never be effective action without unity, without a Liberation Front. The lack of unity is the root of the failure of the popular Angolan uprising.

# BRITAIN AND ANGOLA: THE ATTITUDE OF THE BRITISH GOVERNMENT

## PATRICK WALL

UNTIL recent months, the average Englishman considered the Portuguese colonial policy to be admirable for, although it was known that the Portuguese did not stand any nonsense and that their administration was apt to adopt methods of coercion which would not be acceptable in British Africa, there appeared to be little, if any, discrimination between the races.

Now this picture has been rudely shaken. Reports emanating mainly from British Baptist missionaries in Angola have painted a totally different picture—the full apparatus of a Fascist dictatorship has been created in Angola; the *assimilado* policy was merely a cloak designed to convince the world that the Portuguese were non-racialists. Angola has been exploited to such an extent that the indigenous people were forced to rise in revolt.

Two very different pictures, and perhaps the truth lies somewhere between the two extremes. However, while British citizens may have their own views as to what is happening in Angola, it may be of advantage to consider to what degree these events concern the British Government. It can, after all, be argued that these matters are

PATRICK WALL was an officer in the Royal Marines from 1935–1950 and in 1954 was elected Member of Parliament for Haltemprice in Yorkshire. He became Chairman of the Mediterranean Group of the Conservative Commonwealth Council and Chairman of the Conservative East and Central Africa Committee, and is now a Vice Chairman of the Commonwealth Affairs Committee. He is particularly interested in East and Central Africa which he often visits. From 1955–1960 he was Parliamentary Private Secretary to the Rt. Hon. Derrick Heathcote Amory as Minister of Agriculture and later when Chancellor of the Exchequer.

no concern of ours as Portugal is a Sovereign power and as Britain has always maintained the sanctity of Article 2 (7) of the Charter which prevents the United Nations from interfering in the internal affairs of its members.

## Events in the House of Commons

In February 1961, outbreaks of violence occurred in Angola and in subsequent months a number of Questions were tabled in the House of Commons, based largely on reports from British missionaries—mainly Baptist—serving in that country.

Anxiety about Angola increased and in June the Opposition took the opportunity of a Supply Day (i.e. a day when they have the choice of subject) to debate the proposed despatch of the 19th Brigade to Portugal for training and moved the Adjournment of the House on this matter.

The Opposition's argument was that by sending British troops to Portugal for an exercise at a time when there was acute controversy over the actions of the Portuguese Government in Angola, they were inevitably giving the impression to the world that they supported the colonial policy of that Government. This was denied by Government speakers who maintained that there were sound military reasons why this exercise should take place, that it had been arranged some months previously and that, up to the present, no one had made any protest. It was regarded by the Government purely as a military affair and had nothing whatever to do with the colonial policy of Portugal.

A better opportunity to clarify the views of both Government and Opposition occurred early in July when Mr. Gaitskell moved the Adjournment of the House in order to discuss Angola. In his opening speech he referred to the exceptionally savage character of the repression and the refusal of the Portuguese dictatorship to concede any rights or any hope of advance of self-government to the African peoples. He said that he did not accuse the British Government of indifference to events in Angola but he did accuse

them of having created an extremely bad impression in the
rest of the world. He then cited seven different cases of
voting abstentions in the United Nations; the visit of *H.M.S.
Leopard* to Angola; the visit of the Foreign Secretary to
Lisbon; the 19th Brigade exercise, later called off because
of events in Kuwait; the sale of two frigates to Portugal;
the visit of units of the British fleet to Lisbon and the
refusal of a visa to Captain Galvão. In his reply, the Lord
Privy Seal, Mr. Heath, stated that the situation in Angola
was very serious and that events there had caused the
Government great distress. He pointed out that there were
fundamental differences between the policy pursued in
British Africa and that of Portugal in Angola. He went on
to explain that the exchange of visits that had occurred were
perfectly normal as between NATO allies; that the export
of arms to overseas territories of Portugal had not been
suspended and that there were particular reasons, because
of the terms of the resolution, why the British representative
had abstained in the United Nations. The Government
differed from the Opposition in that when there were differences of opinion between allies they believed that these
should be discussed frankly and in a friendly manner
whereas the Opposition appeared to advocate that we
should cancel any contract and cut adrift from our ally.

Conservative Back Benchers, however, took a much
stronger line than the Lord Privy Seal. Atrocities, wherever
they were committed, were horrible and protests must be
made but these should be consistent; there were not many
protests from the Opposition when one million Moslems
and Hindus were slaughtered in the intercommunal riots
which followed the transfer of power in India and protests
were very much less over the Mau Mau atrocities, or over
similar events in the Congo, than they had been about
Angola. At Question Time, one member of the Opposition had asked whether the Government were proposing to
expel Portugal from NATO. Was any proposal ever made
to expel the Soviet Union from the United Nations after
events in Budapest and did not the Opposition press for the

inclusion of Red China in the Security Council long after the invasion of Tibet when thousands of Tibetans were slaughtered? Another Conservative speaker reminded the House that the first duty of the Portuguese Government was to restore law and order, as we would have had to do had we been in their place. The Portuguese colonial system was quite different from ours; it was based on paternalism and assimilation which were much slower processes; it had, however, worked very well in Goa where the people considered themselves Portuguese and did not want to be anything else.

In winding up, the Opposition spokesman referred to events in Angola as one of the great issues of our time and a human tragedy on an appalling scale; where tens of thousands of men and women and little children, white as well as black, were being killed like cattle. He accused the Government of a prim and bureaucratic approach and of a total failure to appreciate the conditions which produced the events which started with the African rising in February. In replying for the Government, the Minister of State for Foreign Affairs again stressed the fact that the Government did not agree with the Portuguese colonial policy but said that as far as suggestions of Portuguese repression was concerned it was very difficult to get the true facts and that, possibly, a one-sided impression had been painted. Far more information was needed before a true judgment could be reached. In any case, the NATO Alliance and the obligations of that Alliance must continue on a friendly basis and had nothing to do with events in Angola.

## The Facts

What conclusions can be drawn from the morass of charge and counter-charge? Perhaps they can be summarised as follows:

The reason that the Portuguese regard their overseas territories as provinces of Portugal is based on history and not on expediency.

The economic and social development of Angola has

lagged behind other colonial and ex-colonial territories but
Portugal herself is a poor and backward country.

The spirit of Pan-Africanism has directly clashed with
the Portuguese policy of assimilation.

Though officially, and in law, there is little—if any—discrimination between European and African this does exist
in fact and the malpractices associated with the system of
contract labour is especially disliked.

There are far too few schools and the Roman Catholic
Church's appeals in this respect have been largely dis-
regarded. Without adequate education, the African could
not attain full citizenship and gain his just rights.

Freedom of speech and association are curtailed both in
Portugal and her overseas territories and the Secret Police
are feared and disliked.

In spite of the obvious defects of the Portuguese administration, the revolt did not spread and lacked popular
support. It was planned and launched from the Congo and
terrorist bands committed atrocities, and terrorised the
country people, many of whom fled over the border.

Once the Portuguese civilians obtained arms, they hit
back with everything they had. Atrocities have been committed in the early stages by both sides but anti-Portuguese
propaganda has been exaggerated, particularly by certain
missionary organisations. In regaining control the army
were acting lawfully and seem to be carrying out their task
in accordance with International Law.

The Portuguese authorities appear, somewhat belatedly,
to have woken up to the abuses that have been going on and
are now doing their best to have them rectified.

To what extent the Portuguese policy of assimilation, as
opposed to the British system of training the indigenous
people to run their own affairs on local and national levels,
will succeed remains to be seen.

*British Policy*

In a year when Sierra Leone and Tanganyika have become independent members of the Commonwealth, Britain

has clearly demonstrated that she does not agree with the policy of the Portuguese in Africa. Events in the Congo have underlined the disasters that may occur if the indigenous people are not trained to stand on their own feet, both economically and politically. But we, in Britain, recognise that this takes time and that 'too fast' can be as dangerous as 'too slow'.

What happens in Angola is, however, Portugal's affair and unless it affects British subjects or property or has repercussions in British territory, Britain has no right to interfere. The fact that British missionaries were involved and that Angola had become a *cause célèbre* throughout Africa, entitled Britain to make representations to the Portuguese Government.

As our oldest ally and a partner in NATO everything was to be gained by a friendly approach while, at the same time, attempting to insulate the area from supplies of foreign arms, etc. These representations seem to have been effective and there is little evidence to show that the Portuguese army has acted incorrectly once it took over the control from the civilians in the early stages of the revolt. If Portuguese policy in Africa is to be made the excuse for ejecting Portugal from NATO this defensive alliance against the Soviet Union would soon be in ruins and the Soviet Union would have succeeded in all its desires.

As far as the United Nations is concerned, Britain abstained in the Security Council voting in March, partly owing to the fact that we have always upheld Article 2 (7) of the Charter which states:

Nothing contained in the present Charter shall authorise the United Nations to intervene in matters which are essentially within the domestic jurisdiction of any State or shall require the Members to submit such matters to settlement under the present Charter; but this principle shall not prejudice the application of enforcement measures under Chapter VII.

Obviously Angola is within the domestic jurisdiction of Portugal and is, by ancient law, a Province of Portugal. Further, we did not recognise that events in Angola were likely to endanger the maintenance of peace and security and the Security Council has no power to act unless such a situation is seen to exist.

In April, a new resolution was passed by the General Assembly calling the attention of the Portuguese Government to the urgent need for reforms in Angola and setting up a Committee of Enquiry to examine the situation in that country. There were two votes against (Spain and South Africa) and nine abstentions (including Britain) with fourteen countries absent. In June the Security Council passed a further resolution and again Britain abstained but expressed the hope that Portugal would co-operate with the Committee of Enquiry. The debate in the House of Commons in July which has already been referred to, gave the Government an opportunity to present a comprehensive account of its attitude to the problem of Angola which certainly seems to have been justified by subsequent events.

A question mark hangs over the whole continent; the concept of multi-racialism, implying an equal partnership between black and white in spite of the disparity in numbers, stands in ruins. Once the African has political power he will dominate and it remains to be seen whether or not the white settler will be tolerated. Having obtained political power it is clear that African Governments will then seek the transfer of economic power to African hands. Can the white man remain anywhere in Africa except on a temporary basis, as a trader or technical adviser? What is clear is that the white population of central and southern Africa will not give up the rights which they have held, in some cases, for centuries without a struggle. The more enlightened try to bring the African into full partnership but as a junior partner in the knowledge that once power has been transferred, the senior partner is likely to be ejected and the firm made bankrupt.

It is difficult to see the right course. African government in multi-racial countries will bring authoritarian government and probably dictatorship which, at best, would neutralise the continent in the power struggle between East and West and at the worst, would throw large areas into the Communist camp. Is there a middle way, if not, the alternative is indeed a dark one?

# THE OLDEST ALLIANCE
# FACES A CRISIS

## BASIL DAVIDSON

WHAT principles have governed British Ministers in their reaction to the Angolan imbroglio? How have these principles appeared in practice? Where if anywhere in this complex story may one find the logic of current attitudes towards Angola that cut sharply across the general British policy of 'decolonisation' initiated by the Labour Government of 1945, and most ably conducted in recent years by Mr. Iain Macleod?

### The Old Alliance

In attempting a brief answer to these questions, it may be useful to begin with the old treaties. The oldest Anglo-Portuguese treaty of alliance and mutual aid is Plantagenet, and barely relevant; yet even here it is worth noting that the characteristic limits of subsequent behaviour were already defined. When in 1961 the rebellious liberal, Captain Galvão, was refused permission to visit the United Kingdom, he was in fact suffering under Article 3 of the Treaty of Windsor of 1386:

Further it is mutually agreed that it shall not be by any means permitted to the said Kings, or to any of their subjects, Lands or Dominions, of whatsoever station, degree or condition, to give or afford to in any manner counsel, aid or favour any land, Dominion or Nation, which shall be at enmity with or

BASIL DAVIDSON is a well-known writer and journalist, especially on African affairs. His books about Africa include: *Report on Southern Africa* (1952), *The New West Africa* (Editor with A. Ademola of symposium, 1953), *The African Awakening* (Belgian Congo and Angola, 1955), *Old Africa Rediscovered* (1959) and *Black Mother*. During the war Mr. Davidson served as a British liaison officer with partisan forces in Yugoslavia and German-occupied Italy, and was awarded the M.C.

rebelling against either Party . . . or to give directly or indirectly, publicly or clandestinely, any countenance, of whatever kind or nature it may be, to such enemies or rebels . . .
or to administer or extend to such enemies and rebels any
succour that may redound to the prejudice of the other
party . . .

The general terms of this 'oldest alliance' were confirmed
by Charles I in 1642; but the corner-stone of Britain's
modern relations with Portugal—if the adjective be allow-
able in this connexion—was laid with Charles II's Marriage
Treaty of 1661.   Here we find the full doctrine of 'aid
and protection' in formal and unequivocal detail.   Thus
Article 15: 'The King of Great Britain doth profess and
declare, with the consent and advice of his Council, that he
will take the interest of Portugal and all its Dominions to
heart, defending the same with his utmost power by sea
and land even as England itself . . .'  This undertaking
was defined more narrowly in a secret article appended to
the Treaty:

It is by this Secret Article concluded and accorded that His
Majesty of Great Britain in regard of the great advantages
and increase of Dominions he hath purchased by the above-
mentioned Treaty of Marriage shall promise and oblige himself, as by the present article he doth, to defend and protect
all the Conquests and Colonies belonging to the Crown of
Portugal, against all his Enemies, as well future as present:
moreover, His Majesty of Great Britain doth oblige himself
to mediate a good peace between . . . Portugal . . . and the
Dutch upon conditions convenient and becoming the mutual
interests of England and Portugal and in case such peace
ensue not, then His Majesty of Great Britain shall be obliged
to defend, with men and ships, the said Dominions and Conquests of the King of Portugal.[1]

There is no need to enlarge on the political reasons for
this remarkably inclusive alliance: if the Portuguese wished
for protection, the English also desired a useful maritime
ally against the sea-power of the Netherlands.   The fact that
settlements and strong points along the African coast had
become involved (notably, Luanda in Angola and Mozambique Island on the eastern seaboard) was little more than

accidental: the big prizes were farther afield, and they were well worth fighting for.

The alliance persisted. Neither side had reason to disrupt it: each side, from time to time, had cause to be grateful for it. To a later generation the Lines of Torres Vedras seemed to prove the worth of this friendship once and for all. There was Britain and there was Portugal: two maritime nations whose basic principle of policy must always be the same, 'the freedom of the seas', a political reality as well as a toast that could and should be drunk in the splendid liquors of Oporto.

Modern discords on this harmonious theme were struck in the early nineteenth century, with the British attempt to suppress the overseas slave trade. Yet the dissonance was not serious. Humanitarian considerations apart, Britain's chief interest now was to prevent the delivery of African captives to the non-British sugar-producing islands of the West Indies, since these were cutting into the British market with sugar at cheaper prices; but the Portuguese slaving traffic was mainly to Brazil. British impatience with Lisbon grew more pressing a little later, when anti-slavery had become a general watchword and a mark of respectability in international affairs. For the Portuguese were laggards in the cause, and it is not difficult to see why.

In the case of Angola, the greatest colonial possession that Portugal has ever had in Africa (excepting Mozambique in the heyday of the gold trade from the interior), the abolition of slaving and slavery proved hard to achieve. Portuguese planters along the Angolan littoral had welcomed the abolition of the export trade in African captives, because the demands of Brazil had always run counter to their own need for plantation slaves. These settlers were well enough satisfied when the Brazilian demand was finally stopped. But they were bitterly opposed, by the same token, to the abolition of internal slavery. To this they brandished what the *Grande Enciclopédia Portuguesa* has called *grandes e nefastas resistências*.[2] Allowing for this, a Lisbon decree of 1858 declared that internal slavery in all the Portuguese overseas territories should cease in 1878, twenty years later: and in 1869, confirming this liberal measure, there intervened another few years of enlightenment during which, as a Portuguese writer, Senhor da Silva Cunha, has deplored, 'the courts protected the sacred right of idleness'. Yet the settlers had possession on their side, and this was to prove too strong for paper promises in Lisbon.

In 1875, three years before internal slavery in Angola was supposed to end, another decree announced that the ex-slaves were to labour for two years in the service of their ex-owners. As the *Enciclopédia* notes, this was fatal to the emerging principle of 'free labour'—of a 'free market', that is, in which men could try to sell their labour for whatever wages they could get or could combine to get; and the whole notion of a labour market was scrapped, even before it had become a reality, by the *obligation to work*.[3]

Henceforth, this obligation lay at the foundations of all Portuguese colonial policy in Mozambique as well as in Angola (although not, it would appear, in Portuguese Guinea). The decree of 1875 transformed outright slavery into what may be termed 'periodical slavery'. It said, indeed, that only 'declared vagrants' could be compelled to enter into 'labour contracts', but this was inadequate to fill the need for plantation slaves, and in 1899 another decree affirmed that *all natives* were now subject to the obligation, 'moral and legal', to acquire by labour the means of subsisting or of 'bettering their social condition'. This law 'consecrated the principle of forced labour'[4] and has remained in practice, to all intents and purposes, to this day.

These Portuguese attitudes were unwelcome to liberal opinion in London. Seen from there, the grand old Portuguese alliance began to wear a down-at-heel and even shameful appearance: after all, Queen Anne was dead and the Napoleonic wars were long since fought and won.

According to their lights, the Victorians were trying hard
to build a better world; and most of them were sure, no
matter what carping doubt might assail the subversive few,
that they had succeeded tolerably well. It was clearly
time for 'the oldest ally' to reform. But the Portuguese
stubbornly failed to reform or to be reformed, and a
scathing note began to creep into London's communications
with Lisbon. Dr. Hanna has lately recovered a wryly
amusing example of this. At the end of the 1880s the
Lisbon Geographical Society established an Anti-Slavery
League with the King as its patron and blandly declared, in
face of all the evidence, 'that in supporting the mission
inaugurated by Cardinal Lavigerie, Portugal is only carrying out her traditional anti-slaving policy'. This caused
even the British Foreign Office to smile. 'They have dis-
covered', minuted Sir Villiers Lister, 'that the suppression
of slavery is the traditional policy of Portugal. They have
no sense of the ridiculous.'[5]

Yet humanitarian impatience was only part of the trouble
which now began to shake the old alliance: there was also
imperialist impatience. When the Berlin colonial conference formally opened the scramble for Africa, Portuguese claims to the whole 'middle belt' from the Atlantic
in Angola to the Indian Ocean in Mozambique, with all
that lay between, were at last submitted to practical tests
of who could 'occupy' and who could not. The Portuguese,
of course, were incapable of meeting these tests except in
western Angola and in eastern Mozambique, and up the
Zambezi as far as Tete. Hitherto, these Portuguese claims
to the whole of 'middle Africa', however empty, had suited
Britain well enough, for they had placed a huge segment
of the unexplored continent under the loose 'suzerainty'
of a small power which was generally accepted as being
under British protection. But what suited Britain failed
to suit France and Germany; nor did it suit King Leopold
of the Belgians, now fully embarked on his curious
adventure in the Congo basin. The French and Germans

supported Leopold's claim to both banks of the Congo estuary, and the British found themselves obliged to fight a rearguard action on behalf of the Portuguese. This they did without pleasure. A contemporary despatch from *The Times'* correspondent in Berlin shows how the alliance now received its first serious dent in Africa.

Tonight I have to announce what is probably the most solid result of the West African Conference—namely, the final settlement of the various territorial claims to the lower portion of the Congo ... The Conference has only been kept waiting by the obstinacy of the Lisbon Cabinet, which seemed determined to have its own selfish way in respect to the Lower Congo, but after various remedies in the nature of *douce violence* had been vainly employed by the Powers interested in the success of King Leopold's undertaking, the Portuguese Cabinet was at last induced to give way, under the pressure of identical notes from France, England and Germany . . .[6]

The Portuguese, as it turned out, were fortunate to keep as much of Africa as they did, for they had nothing but a notional 'occupation' to support their imperial claim to vast lands in east and west. Yet Britain, once she had secured the greater part of the central plateau and the mineral wealth which was believed (not wrongly) to lie there, was well enough content to revert to a policy of protecting 'Portuguese conquests' which added what was often thought of (and again not wrongly) as a large appendix to her own empire in middle Africa.

The policy of protection was none the less to be sorely undermined in the years immediately ahead. It seemed doubtful whether Portugal could really hold these vast territories. It appeared more than possible that she would either let them slip or basely sell them to the highest bidder. London looked suspiciously at France (then deep in collusion with Leopold and his Congo Free State), and put a careful rod in pickle. In 1898 Mr. Balfour signed a secret agreement with Count Hatzfeld which divided the Portuguese colonies in Africa into spheres of influence between Britain and Germany. Prince Lichnowsky, afterwards

German Ambassador in London, has told the story.[7] Commenting on this secret agreement, he wrote in 1916 (as part of an apologia for having failed to prevent the War), that:

As the Government of Portugal had neither the power nor the means to open up her extended possessions or to administer them properly, she had already thought of selling them before and thus relieving her financial burdens. An agreement had been come to between us and England which defined the interests of both parties, and which was of the greater value because Portugal is entirely dependent on England, as is generally known.

On the face of it this agreement was to safeguard the integrity and independence of the Portuguese State, and merely declared the intention of being of financial and economic assistance to the Portuguese. Literally, therefore, it did not contravene the ancient Anglo-Portuguese Alliance . . .

The Portuguese Government thought otherwise. Whatever they believed they might have to do about their African colonies, they were certainly not going to admit any intermediate diminution of their sovereignty. To put it at the lowest point, admission of an Anglo-German economic suzerainty over their colonies would have meant forfeiture of their hope of selling, if they were eventually bound to sell, in the most favourable market. They accordingly asked for a formal restatement of the Anglo-Portuguese Alliance, and this was made by the Treaty of Windsor of 1899—the very year, as we have seen, when the principle of forced labour for all Africans was 'consecrated' in Angola. The new Treaty merely confirmed the old agreements but it caused disappointment, not to say irritation, in Berlin.

Anglo-German negotiations were resumed in 1912, with Lichnowsky now Germany's ambassador in London. He goes on:

The object of negotiations between us and England, which had commenced before my arrival, was to amend and improve our agreement of 1898, as it had proved unsatisfactory on several points as regards geographical delimitation. Thanks to the accommodating attitude of the British Government I succeeded in making the new agreement fully accord with our wishes and interests. The whole of Angola up to the 20th degree of longitude was assigned to us,* so that we stretched up to the Congo State from the south ; we also acquired the valuable islands of San Thomé and Principe, which are north of the Equator and therefore really in the French sphere of influence, a fact which caused my French colleague to enter strong but unavailing protests.

Further, we obtained the northern part of Mozambique ; the Licango formed the border.

The British Government showed the greatest consideration for our interests and wishes. Sir E. Grey intended to demonstrate his goodwill towards us, but he also wished to assist our colonial development as a whole, as England hoped to divert the German development of strength from the North Sea and Western Europe to the Ocean and to Africa. 'We don't want to grudge Germany her colonial development', a member of the Cabinet said to me.

The British Government originally intended to include the Congo State in the agreement, which would have given us the right of pre-emption and enabled us to penetrate it economically. We refused this offer nominally in view of Belgian susceptibilities. Perhaps we wished to be economical of successes? With regard also to the practical realisation of its real though unexpressed intention—the later actual partition of the Portuguese colonies—the treaty in its new form showed marked improvements and advantages as compared with the old one. Cases had been specified which empowered us to take steps to guard our interests in the districts assigned to us. These were couched in such a manner that it was really left to us to decide when 'vital' interests arose, so that, with Portugal entirely dependent on England, it was only necessary to cultivate further good relations with England in order to carry out our joint intentions at a later date with English assent.

In the event, this partition agreement proved abortive. War broke out before it could be signed, and the holocaust of 1914–18 carried it away beyond recall. But I have quoted these extensive passages here for the useful light they throw on the practical significance of the Anglo-Portuguese alliance in its imperialist bearing on Africa. Despite contempt for Portuguese administration, successive British Governments preferred that Portugal should have Angola and Mozambique; but if Portugal could not hold

* That is to say, about four-fifths of Angola.

them they were to be divided between Britain and Germany to the disadvantage of France and Leopold.

Having thus set the traditional scene, and sketched the historical background to British attitudes in 1961, let us pass to modern times.

## Between the Wars and After

After 1918 there were no more attempts to provide against a possible Portuguese collapse in Africa. Most of the Anglo-Portuguese colonial frontiers had been settled in 1891; with one or two modifications they remained intact. The colonial pattern had settled down. The French were busy in West Africa. The Germans were out of the running. And Mozambique and Angola, by the twenties, had become politically convenient and economically useful to British imperial interests.

Yet little capital was invested. A British consortium headed by the late Sir Robert Williams obtained a ninety-nine years' concession in 1902 for the construction of a railway from Central Africa to the Atlantic. Work began on this 838-mile railway in 1903 but was completed only in 1928, while the connecting rail link to the Katanga was not opened until 1931. Since then the Benguela Railway, as this remarkable undertaking was named, has functioned as a useful transporter of minerals from the Katanga, although to a much lesser extent—owing to the rivalry of the Beira Railway to the East Coast—as a transporter of minerals from Northern Rhodesia. Owned as to nine-tenths by Tanganyika Concessions Ltd., the Railway was thought to have a golden future and results have often confirmed this anticipation. Net profits for 1960, for example, amounted to £994,247, or rather more than one quarter of the total net profits of Tanganyika Concessions during that year.

Diamonds have so far proved to be Angola's most profitable mineral. They are worked by the Companhia de Diamantes de Angola in which, despite its name, the Portuguese have only a minority holding. Sole diamond rights over some 390,000 square miles of Angola (which has a total of 481,351 square miles) were secured for fifty years in 1921; but half the net profits were to be allocated to the colonial government of the territory. In 1959, for example, the Angolan Government received about 106 million escudos from this valuable source.

A few other British firms have acquired interests in Angola. Companhia de Combustiveis, a British enterprise, owns a bulk oil installation at Lobito. Walford Lines have an Angolan subsidiary, Hull, Blyth and Co., coal and oil contractors and shipping agents, also have a business in Angola; and there are a few other relatively small British investments.

The position in Mozambique shows a number of British trading and shipping firms with useful subsidiaries; but there the principal outside interest is that of the Rand goldmines. They import large quantities of mining labour by special agreement with the Mozambique authorities; and it appears that the present cheap-labour structure of Rand mining could not be supported without these workers.

Such comparatively modest interests could not possibly reform an economy which lingered in the nineteenth century and seemed powerless to shift itself forward. But they lent the appearance of a useful commercial partnership to the pretensions of the old alliance; and this seems to have been enough to confirm the traditional view in Whitehall that Portuguese positions should be automatically defended against any other Power in Europe, or indeed elsewhere. Moreover, the colonies of all the powers in Africa were more or less completely stagnant, and seemed likely to remain so. Why should Angola be any different? It might well be that the administration of Angola was somewhat more old-fashioned than that of neighbouring territories; but could this be seriously thought to matter? Outside a narrow business circle, and the even narrower society of those who read consular reports, little or nothing was known or thought or written about Angola; the country was believed, like most of Africa, to lie in hopeless slumber behind insurmountable barriers of irredeemable inferiority.

This indifference was pierced now and then by angry words from missionaries and humanitarian reporters. Henry Nevinson wrote his *A Modern Slavery*.[8]  William Cadbury made his personal investigation of forced labour on the cocoa islands of San Thomé and Principe, and began an eventually successful campaign to stop the big chocolate firms from buying their cocoa from the Portuguese.[9] John Harris trod the same road.[10]  But the business connexions and the 'old alliance' were generally too strong for them.  There never arose in Britain any great movement of protest against forced labour in Angola such as could compare with the enormously influential Congo Reform Association, founded by E. D. Morel and others in 1904 to campaign against the Leopoldian Congo.  Outside the ranks of journalism and religion the only clear voice that was raised against the comparable brutalities of the Portuguese in Angola was that of William Cadbury.  There could scarcely be a more persuasive witness to the power of traditional diplomacy, for the evidence pointed beyond any doubt to a situation in Angola where chattel slavery was perpetuated on a massive scale—sanctioned, moreover, by the law—in a 'periodical slavery' which might be labelled, *para ingles ver,* 'contract labour' but was none the less a pitiless form of servitude.

After the First World War there was some improvement. General Norton de Mattos, a former Governor of the territory, returned to Angola as High Commissioner and with instructions to conduct an ambitious programme of development and colonisation.  A year later, thanks to the intelligent pressure of de Mattos and the willingness of the Republican Government in Lisbon to give a blessing to any effort that should try to lift Angola out of its wretchedness, the colonial administration was debarred from recruiting African labour for private employers—since this practice as was declared at the time, had 'led to abuses'.  In 1925 the Republican Government actually voted the relatively generous sum of £2 millions (its equivalent, that is, i escudos) to pay for a number of urgently needed public works; but the same year, unfortunately, brought a partial return to the old system of labour recruiting for private as well as state enterprises. In the words of the *Encyclopaedia Britannica*, chiefs were 'required to produce the men, and both chiefs and officials received payment per head for the labour obtained'.[11] And then the Republic fell, and Dr. Salazar, whose ideas were strictly authoritarian, came to power. The liberal efforts of de Mattos were discontinued or deliberately condemned: Angola declined still further into slumbering misery.

Here, of course, one should remember the 'colonial atmosphere' of the thirties and forties. They were years of great discouragement of change in any part of Africa. With one or two exceptions in West Africa and rare manifestations elsewhere, little or nothing of the ferment of Indian nationalism could be found. Even the whites of Africa, more often than not, were fighting for their lives against the ruinous effects of world depression, against an utter want of capital and against poverty of every kind and to which few could see a likely end. The jagged turmoil of European invasion—completed in Angola, as often elsewhere, only in the twenties—appeared to have run itself into a hopeless *cul-de-sac* of frustration and futility.

Britain knew little of Angola in the thirties and forties, and certainly cared still less. But from the early fifties, and for many reasons which are out of context here, Africa moved steadily and rapidly into the centre of world attention, and therefore into the centre of British attention. Reports from Angola aroused a new interest. To those who watched Africa with care, it was now that this vast territory began to seem peculiarly eccentric to the developing situation in the continent. Elsewhere the old habits of using Africans as forced labour for public or private purposes had generally disappeared, at any rate as habits that were fundamental to the colonial system; and the foundations of an industrial and urban revolution had begun to appear. Cities grew enormously in population as villagers

flocked to the centres of wage labour and a new indus-
trialism. Social services were launched. Schools were
extended. British and French universities began to fill with
students from the African colonies. Change and growth
were in the air. But not in Angola.

It is vital to understand this contrast between Angola and
its neighbouring countries, in order to comprehend both
the nature of Angolan nationalism and the dilemma of
loyalty in which Britain was soon to be plunged. Some of
the evidence may be useful here, even in a journalistically
potted form. Thus a travelling correspondent of the *New
York Herald-Tribune,* writing of Angola in the issue of
15 February 1948, noted of the labour system that: 'When
an Angola plantation owner requires labour, he notifies the
Government of his needs. The demand is passed down to
the village chiefs, who are ordered to supply fixed quotas
of labourers from their communities. If the required
number is not forthcoming, police are sent to round them
up.' Now it was a relevant fact, noted at the time, that
only in Portuguese Africa was any such system of coercion
still in force on any significant scale.

Next, in 1955, there was published in London a transla-
tion of extracts from a deeply disturbing report made eight
years earlier by an Inspector-General of Oversea Territories,
Captain Henrique Galvão. After extensive travels in
Angola, and access to records both official and confidential,
Captain Galvão felt it his duty to report to the Government
of Dr. Salazar that the situation in Angola was tragic and
disgraceful. He laid stress on the abuses of the law with
regard to colony-wide impressment of forced labour. He
considered that the worst aspect of the labour position

lay in the attitude of the State to the recruitment of labour
for private employers. Here the position is worse in Angola
than in Mozambique; because in Angola, openly and deliberately, the State acts as recruiting and distributing agent for
labour on behalf of settlers who, as though it were quite
natural, write to the Department of Native Affairs for 'a
supply of workers'. The word 'supply' [*fornecer*] is used
indifferently of goods or of men.[12]

After describing methods of recruitment of forced labour —labelled, as previously, 'contract labour'—Galvão continued:

In some ways the situation is worse than simple slavery. Under slavery, after all, the Native is bought as an animal: his owner prefers him to remain as fit as a horse or an ox. Yet here the Native is not bought—he is hired from the State, although he is called a free man. And his employer cares little if he sickens or dies, once he is working, because when he sickens or dies his employer will simply ask for another.

That was in 1947. In 1954 the present writer, after interviewing half a dozen principal employers of labour in such centres as Lobito, Catumbela and Luanda—all of whom were using 'contract labour'—was informed by the head of the Department of Native Affairs in Luanda that the total number of 'contract workers' was no fewer than 379,000, or nearly one-tenth of the whole African population of the territory.[13]    A year later Mr. John Gunther, the American reporter, basing himself mainly on experience in Mozambique, declared that 'the worst thing about Portuguese Africa is forced labour. Not only does this still exist; the Portuguese authorities admit that it exists, say that it is necessary, and even a "good thing" for its victims, and condone it . . . It is not quite—but almost—a form of slavery.'[14]    Other reports by British and American travellers have since confirmed the general truth of these observations both for Angola and for Mozambique. It was the persuasive consistency of all these testimonies that placed the British Government in an embarrassedly defensive position when it came, in 1961, to defending British friendship for Dr. Salazar's Government.

## The Revolt

The revolt of 1961 is described elsewhere in this volume. By then, indeed, it was quite clear that Portuguese policies were fairly well known and understood in Britain, and that no responsible individual had any thought of defending them. Lisbon's response to British criticism might still be— as before—an outburst of hysterical indignation, generally inferring that the critics were liars, scoundrels or agents of subversion. Yet the fact remains that what was written by individual critics in this country was also thought—and I am giving away no secrets here—by those who conducted and administered the colonial policies of Britain. When official Portuguese argued, as they did increasingly, that they really had the interests of 'their' Africans at heart, and stood indeed at the forefront of wise administration in Africa, the official reaction in London may generally be said to have echoed, though in private, the comment of Sir Villiers Lister some eighty years earlier: 'They have no sense of the ridiculous.'

It was this British awareness of the true nature of Portuguese policy in Angola that gave the Parliamentary exchanges of 1961 their peculiar air of shamed embarrassment. Let us turn now to the record of debates, recalling as we do so the two essential dates: 4 February 1961, when the revolt began, and 15 March, when the main fighting, the massacre of several hundred Europeans and the mass extermination of many thousands of Africans, which began in the Bakongo country. We shall see that the 'old alliance' still held curiously firm, but that the foundations were more than a little shaken.

We can begin on 15 May. Mr. Paget asked Mr. Orr-Ewing, Civil Lord of the Admiralty, whether he would make a statement on the goodwill visit of *H.M.S. Leopard* to Luanda. The Civil Lord explained the circumstances of the visit, passed it off as nothing exceptional, but then, doubtless knowing full well why the Labour Opposition was interested in the movements of a small warship in remote African waters, went on to add:

I welcome the opportunity to emphasise that this visit, which was planned last February, is not connected with colonial policy. To cancel it at this time would have been an insult to a friendly nation and a NATO ally.

To a supplementary from Mr. Brockway, he countered:

I am well aware of the serious position in Angola. That is why we considered the matter of possible cancellation. The

Opposition should bear in mind whether the cancellation of the visit would have done more harm than the continuation of the visit.[15]

A month later, on a Labour adjournment to discuss the projected despatch to Portugal, for training purposes, of the 19th Bde. Group, Mr. Harold Watkinson, the Minister of Defence, conducted himself along the same lines as Mr. Orr-Ewing. Answering Mr. Paget, he said:

The position of the Government is this. We do not agree with Portugal's policy in Africa. This exercise [of the 19th Bde. Gp.] does not in any degree imply that we do agree. We have not condoned what is happening in Africa [he was referring, of course, to Angola], and when we spoke in the United Nations we took the same line as my Right Hon. and Hon. Friends have taken in this House. My Right Hon. Friend the Foreign Secretary made his position and that of the Government perfectly plain in Lisbon. Therefore, I am perfectly entitled to say that this exercise has no political connotations.

Later in his speech, he added:

I want it to be plain, without any shadow of doubt, that our relations with Portugal are the relations that we should have with a NATO ally. We have always made it plain, and I make it plain again now, that this does not imply that we agree in any sense with the colonial policy of the Portuguese. (*Interruption*). This does not, and should not, affect our relations with them as a NATO ally. If we accept this kind of policy, as my Hon. Friend the Member for Windsor asked, where will it stop? What other nations will be involved? The whole of the NATO alliance would be damaged beyond repair.[16]

British relations, we may note, were no longer to be conducted in line with the 'old alliance', but with NATO. The argument that Portugal was a valuable member of NATO, and should therefore be protected no matter what her Government might do in Africa, was none the less carried through with great consistency. A few weeks earlier, on 15 May (and I shall consider the position in the United Nations a little further on), the British Consul in São Paolo was instructed by the Home Office to refuse a British visa to

Captain Galvão, now one of the leaders of the democratic opposition to Dr. Salazar. (Landing at London Airport at the end of the following October, Captain Galvão was again refused entry). On 26 May, moreover, Lord Home, the Foreign Secretary, had paid a goodwill visit to Dr. Salazar in Lisbon, being duly present at the anniversary celebrations of Dr. Salazar's *coup d'état*.

Against mounting criticism in Britain from the Labour and Liberal Parties, from individual Conservatives and from many individuals and bodies who were outside party politics altogether, the Government stood firm for its policy of protecting Dr. Salazar. On 16 June, six British frigates of the Home Fleet anchored in the Tagus after joint exercises with units of the Portuguese navy and air force. On 17 June the British Government announced the sale to Portugal of two frigates, *Mounts Bay* and *Morecambe Bay*.

Yet criticism, now on an international scale and especially strong in Africa and India, had some effect. On 21 June the Norwegian Foreign Minister, Mr. Halvard Lange, declared that his Government had refused to sell ammunition to Portugal. 'Norway', he explained, 'regards it as a burden for the whole western alliance that one member country seeks to retain colonies by use of armed force'.[17] A month later the British Government made a small retreat in the same direction. During an interesting Commons exchange on 4 July about British arms supply to Portugal, Mr. Harold Macmillan observed:

As I said to the House some days ago, the position is that no licences for the export of arms or ammunition from Britain are, in fact, being made in respect of Angola and Mozambique. That does not affect certain large deliveries of equipment that are only suitable for Portugal in her place as a NATO ally.[18]

Yet it seemed hard to draw the line between what was suitable for Portugal as a NATO ally and what was suitable for her in the conduct of colonial war. Which side of the line, for example, would napalm bombs fall? There was strong evidence by now that napalm was being used by the Portuguese in Angola.

Asked by Mr. Hugh Gaitskell what was the point of putting an embargo on the export of arms to Angola when arms could go freely to Portugal and be sent from there to Angola, the Prime Minister replied that: 'In giving these licences, such is the great width and variety of arms that are likely to be asked for that I think that it is quite possible to operate this policy effectively'. Members were left to make the best they could of this sibylline utterance. A full-dress debate on the following day took matters little further.

Britain's voting record at the United Nations has shown the same devious embarrassment. Though unwilling to give the Portuguese any open protection, the British Government appear to have remained* even more unwilling to join in any criticism: the result was an equivocal abstention which was tantamount to covert protection for Lisbon. Thus on 15 March the British delegate helped to obstruct a Security Council resolution calling for reforms in Portugal's African territories. On 20 April the British delegate abstained on a similar resolution in the General Assembly. This resolution was passed by seventy-three votes with two against (Spain and South Africa) and nine abstentions, among the latter being France, Belgium and the Netherlands as well as Britain. On 9 June Britain again abstained on a Security Council resolution critical of Portugal.

It is, after all, an undistinguished record. So long as criticism of Portugal's conduct in Angola remained silent or of small volume, the British Government continued to support Salazar as though nothing had happened. Pressed by rising criticism, Ministers became defensive. Pressed again, they gave way a little. Pressed still harder, they dug in their heels and stood by Salazar even after the United States had abandoned public support of him.

Those who defended this attitude generally took the line that there was nothing else that Britain could honourably

*At least up to the middle of November.

do. We were bound by treaty: moreover, who could be sure that the rebels in Angola were not inspired by Communist or other evil influences? Further, had not Ministers done their best to knock some sense into the heads of those who were conducting policy in Lisbon? 'What is necessary', Lord Home had publicly declared in Lisbon on 25 May, 'is a programme of social and economic advance which is seen by the people to be a reality and a political goal which rallies people to carry responsibility and inspires them with all that is good in patriotism'.

Such arguments failed to convince even those critics who were outside the ranks of the official Opposition. For these arguments seemed to imply that Britain should support Portugal no matter what kind of regime was in power and no matter how degrading of humanity its policies might be: or, alternatively, that Portugal's value to the Western Alliance was such that Britain could not possibly afford to offend Salazar. Then why, it was asked, does America make no difficulty about offending him? Why give comfort to Salazar when every influential non-white voice in the Commonwealth is joined in outright condemnation of him?

Another line of criticism is worth noting for its possibly considerable relevance to any final explanation of the British Government's attitude. Some have believed that what was now thought vital in the Portuguese alliance was no longer any question concerning NATO in its global strategy, but rather the special contribution that Portugal could make to a particular concept of 'strategic security' south of the Sahara. Here, it was affirmed, Britain was in fact supporting Portugal in order to bolster and confirm the pattern of white domination throughout central-southern Africa.

The evidence for this view is interesting. The Federal Government of Rhodesia and Nyasaland, for example, has never concealed its eagerness to support Salazar. In June it sent its Defence Minister, Mr. Caldicott, for talks in Luanda with General Deslandes, the Governor-General of Angola. An obviously inspired comment on these talks, reproduced in a *Daily Telegraph* despatch from Luanda on 28 June, explained that: 'Rhodesia considers Angola of great strategic and political significance to the future of both central and southern Africa. It feels it is of the utmost importance that the territory should remain in friendly hands'. This, of course, was directly along the line of Sir Roy Welensky's often expressed conviction that African nationalism is never more than a tool of Communist subversion: an argument which allows him to maintain, as no other argument could, that continued white supremacy is vital to Western interests in central-southern Africa. African nationalists in this area, and elsewhere, have tended to suspect or conclude that London's stubborn defence of Salazar has owed an important part of its consistency to proddings from Salisbury, Southern Rhodesia, allied to pressure in the Conservative Party from those who have repeatedly assailed the whole policy of decolonisation. It seems likely that some of the vehemence and conviction with which the British Government has been attacked in Africa for 'upholding Tshombe in the Katanga' has come from a belief that Britain, Portugal, the Union of South Africa, Belgium and the Federal Government of Rhodesia and Nyasaland are privately involved in a joint effort to save the substance of white domination throughout the central-southern region.

It is hard to say how far this belief has gained ground in Africa, but my own opinion, for what this may be worth, is that it has lately gained a great deal of ground; and to this extent, of course, Britain cannot but lose the advantage of her forward-looking moves elsewhere. For it places Britain in an equivocal light in which the policy of decolonisation appears no more than a cynical calculation of narrow national interest.

Broadly, though, the main attack in Britain itself has followed a simpler course. There has first of all been a moral objection: if it is wrong to vote for Salazar at the United Nations—even while acting, at home, as though we *had* voted for him—it must also be wrong to abstain from voting against him. It must be wrong to stand aside and encourage evil to complete its work, since no alliance can ever oblige a partner to dishonourable courses. What Mr. Macmillan's critics have felt under this moral heading—what they appear to have felt, above all, about Britain's abstentions in voting at the United Nations—may probably be summed up in a verse of Sir Francis Meynell's for 'a Labourite poet who said before an election that he would abstain':

> The guilty formula still stands;
> To Innocence condemned we owe it.
> Pontius Pilate washed his hands;
> 'I will not vote', said Pontius Poet.

The critics have also entered a political objection. They have said that the Government's equivocation and effective backing for Salazar has made, and is making, the worst of both worlds. It must be harmful to Britain's reputation in a Portugal whose regime can survive only by suppressing its every opponent. It must be still more harmful to Britain's reputation in an Africa where the continuance or desirability of Portuguese rule now appears a matter of the utmost doubt.

And it is perhaps this last point which has seemed most persuasive. For even if it were true—the critics have argued—that national interest need take no account of morality but only of material advantage, where is the advantage in ruining our influence with the emergent nations of the world for the brief benefit of an elderly dictator? What material advantage rests in political futility?

The right course, the critics have maintained, is to help the peoples of Portugal and Angola towards a constructive solution of their problems. This would mean practical British aid for the foundation—no doubt through the agency of the United Nations—of an independent Angola in which every man and woman should at last have a legal and reasonable claim to equality of rights. And why not give such aid? Why not embark upon a modern policy towards an African country whose fate is inextricably woven with the future of its neighbours?   If it was proper seventy-five years ago for Britain to apply *douce violence* to the Govern- of Portugal in the dubious cause of Leopold of Belgium, and thus subtract from Portuguese sovereignty (however well 'attested' by history) the mouth and estuary of the Congo River, why should it be wrong or impracticable to apply such pressure to the Government of Portugal today— and for a far better cause?   If it was justifiable for Britain, fifty years ago, to meet Portuguese official incompetence by arranging to annex a fifth of Angola and for Germany to take the rest, then surely it must now be many times more justifiable to help the peoples of Angola to acquire their own country?

A straight-forward British declaration in favour of Angolan independence could only be beneficial to Angola, and hence to British interests in Africa.   It could only be beneficial to Portugal as well; for then, but only then, the Portuguese genius for social synthesis among widely differing peoples could at last make a significant and memorable contribution towards the renaissance of Africa.

## NOTES

[1] *State Papers,* vol. 1, part 1, pp. 470.

[2] *Grande Enciclopédia Portuguesa e Brasiliera,* vol. 2, p. 611.

[3] Ibid, p. 648.

[4] E. W. Smith reviewing J. M. da Silva Cunha, *O Trabalho Indigena,* Lisbon 1949: *Africa* No. 21 of 1951.

[5] A. J. Hannah, *The Beginnings of Nyasaland and N. E. Rhodesia 1859–85,* London 1956, p. 129.

[6] *The Times,* 15 February 1885.

[7] Prince Lichnowsky, *My Mission to London* (with preface by Professor Gilbert Murray), London 1918.

[8] H. W. Nevinson, *A Modern Slavery,* London 1906.

[9] W. A. Cadbury, *Labour in Portuguese West Africa,* London 1910.

[10] J. H. Harris, *Portuguese Slavery ; Britain's Dilemma,* London 1913.

[11] *Encyclopaedia Britannica,* vol. 1, 1929, pp. 951.

[12] B. Davidson, *The African Awakening,* 1955, pp. 204.

[13] Ibid, p. 196.
[14] J. Gunther, *Inside Africa*, London 1955, p. 574.
[15] *Hansard*, 15 May 1961, cols. 925 onwards.
[16] *Hansard*, 15 June 1961, cols. 769 onwards.
[17] *The Times*, 22 June 1961.
[18] *Hansard*, 4 July 1961, cols. 1256 onwards.
[19] Sir Francis Meynell, *Poems and Pieces, 1911 to 1961*, London 1961, p. 51.